WOMEN ATHLETES AND ENTREPRENEURS: AN EXPLORATORY,

COMPARATIVE STUDY BETWEEN WOMEN BARREL RACERS AND WOMEN

WHO OWN THEIR OWN BUSINESSES

by

Melissa L. Greer, Ph.D.

JOSEPH LEVESQUE, Ph.D., Faculty Mentor and Chair

BARBARA BAILEY, Ph.D., Committee Member

ROSEMARIE LAMM, Ph.D., Committee Member

Kurt Linberg, Ph.D., Dean, School of Business & Technology

A Dissertation Presented in Partial Fulfillment

Of the Requirements for the Degree

Doctor of Philosophy

Capella University

October 2007

AuthorHouse™
1663 Liberty Drive, Suite 200
Bloomington, IN 47403
www.authorhouse.com
Phone: 1-800-839-8640

First published by AuthorHouse 2/2/2009

ISBN: 978-1-4389-1274-5 (sc)

Printed in the United States of America
Bloomington, Indiana

This book is printed on acid-free paper.

Abstract

Sports athletes are connected to business entrepreneurship due to the relationships of business strategies, psychological, and motivational characteristics according to authoritative research. Barrel racing has become a limitless opportunity for success becoming the second favorite event in the rodeo. However, the barrel-racing cowgirl faces criticisms, perhaps, due to a psychic prison that society continues to live from the lack of knowledge of this type of culture. It is debated this industry is not an efficient entrepreneurship endeavor. However, the woman barrel racer is a sports athlete who participates in her own activity to obtain capital, self-actualization, and achievement. It is further acknowledged she is responsible for her own financial resources to pay for business expenses in order to continue the venture. Cowboys have been studied and confirmed to be entrepreneurs so why would women barrel racers be different? The purpose of this study was to compare and contrast Women Barrel Racers (also referred as World Athlete Entrepreneurs) with Women Business Entrepreneurs and determine if there is an association between women who race and women who have their own businesses. The main areas of concern were business strategies, psychological traits, and motivational characteristics. This study also investigated the Birth Theory and the Only or Eldest Daughter Syndrome. Finally, barriers experienced by World Athlete Entrepreneurs and Women Business Entrepreneurs were analyzed. Twenty-five World Athlete Entrepreneurs and twenty-five Women Business Entrepreneurs completed a questionnaire designed by the researcher and the Edwards Personal Preference Schedule in order to investigate nine questions that navigated this study. Analysis of the data discovered three of the five main concerns were in concurrence of past research studies. The results revealed (a) an association of 13 out of 14 psychological characteristics evaluated, (b) an association of motivational characteristics, and (c) an association of business strategies. Further findings reveal this study collaborates with past studies regarding the Birth Theory but not the Only or Eldest Daughter Syndrome. Finally, the data analysis affirmed two of the three impediments explored were congruent with both (a) other research and (b) this study.

Dedication

To the women barrel racers, keep your chins up and continue to turn n' burn for you are World Athlete Entrepreneurs.

To my daughter, Desiree, thank you for all your help and being understanding while I completed this study. You are a great daughter. Always remember that anything can be achieved if you put your heart and soul into it and do not let anyone tell you otherwise. Stay away from negativity and do not let it get in the path of what you want to achieve. I am really proud of you.

To my husband, thank you for not giving up on me while I completed this education.We celebrate 17 years of marriage. We have experienced many ups and downs that life has to offer; however, we have conquered the downs together. Everything you have done and do for me is greatly acknowledged and appreciated.

To my parents, thank you for your continuous love and support you have shown my family and I. There are not enough words to describe the extensive amount of gratitude that is felt for you both. I could not have done this without you two. Thank you for sticking with me and always being there when I needed you. In addition, you are now celebrating 40 years of marriage. Congratulations on this magnificent achievement. I know there will be many more happy years celebrated.

Acknowledgments

Extensive gratitude goes to:

1. Dr. Levesque, my committee chair for continuously being supportive and working with me in order to complete this. Thank you for your time, aspiration, and enthusiasm.

2. Dr. Barbara Bailey, committee member, for being with me since day one of my PhD venture. You have been a great inspiration to me. Thank you for your time, aspiration, and enthusiasm.

3. Dr. Rosemarie Lamm, outside scholar committee member, thank you for the continuous feedback and educational support you provided. Thank you for taking the time out of your busy schedule to meet with me when you were engaged with your regular students. Thank you for your time, aspiration, and enthusiasm.

4. David Edwards, the trustee of the estate for Allen Edwards, author of the Edwards Personal Preference Schedule, for the permission of allowing me to use the test for this study.

5. The women barrel racers and women business entrepreneurs from all over the United States who took the time from their busy schedules to respond to the data collection instruments in order to create the data, in which these findings were made. Thank you for your time, aspiration, and enthusiasm.

6. The subscribers to the Florida Equine Athlete (Florida Barrel Racer's Journal) publication. Thank you for your help, patience, and understanding when the publication was running late in production in order for this to be completed.

Table of Contents

Dedication iii

Acknowledgments iv

List of Tables x

List of Figures xii

CHAPTER 1. INTRODUCTION 1

Introduction to the Problem 1

Background 2

Statement of the Problem 3

The Purpose 4

Rationale 5

Research Questions 6

Significance of the Study 7

Definition of Terms 7

Assumptions and Limitations 10

Nature of the Study 11

Organization of the Remainder of the Study 12

CHAPTER 2. LITERATURE REVIEW 13

Introduction 13

CHAPTER 3. METHODOLOGY   26

    Design of the Study   27

    Population and Sample   29

    Instrumentation   30

    Data Collection   30

    Data Analysis   31

    Ethical Considerations   33

    Questionnaire Design   34

    Privacy and Confidentiality   34

    Validity and Reliability   35

CHAPTER 4. DATA COLLECTION AND ANALYSIS   36

CHAPTER 5. RESULTS, CONCLUSIONS, AND RECOMMENDATIONS   70

    Summary   82

    Recommendations   84

REFERENCES   88

APPENDIX A. DATA COLLECTION INSTRUMENT – WAE QUESTIONNAIRE   92

APPENDIX B. DATA COLLECTION INSTRUMENT – WBE QUESTIONNAIRE   95

APPENDIX C. INFORMED CONSENT LETTER   98

APPENDIX D. RECRUITMENT INFORMATION   101

APPENDIX E. ACHIEVEMENT VARIABLE CHI – SQUARE TEST   102

APPENDIX F. CHANGE VARIABLE CHI-SQUARE TEST   103

APPENDIX G. CONFIDENCE CHI-SQUARE TEST   104

APPENDIX H. DOMINANCE VARIABLE CHI – SQUARE TEST   105

APPENDIX I. FLEXIBILITY VARIABLE CHI-SQUARE TEST   106

APPENDIX J. TO FULFILL A PASSION VARIABLE CHI – SQUARE TEST   107

APPENDIX K. SENSE OF SELF-VARIABLE CHI-SQUARE TEST   108

APPENDIX L. ABILITY TO UTILIZE A SKILL OR TALENT CHI-SQUARE TEST   109

APPENDIX M. MARITAL STATUS CHI-SQUARE TESTS - MARRIED VARIABLE   110

APPENDIX N. MARITAL STATUS CHI-SQUARE TESTS - DIVORCED VARIABLE   111

APPENDIX O. MARITAL STATUS CHI-SQUARE TESTS - SEPARATED VARIABLE   112

APPENDIX P. MARITAL STATUS CHI-SQUARE TESTS - SINGLE VARIABLE   113

APPENDIX Q. EPPS PSYCHOLOGICAL CHARACTERISTICS CROSS TABULATIONS - ABASEMENT VARIABLE   114

APPENDIX R. EPPS PSYCHOLOGICAL CHARACTERISTICS CROSS TABULATIONS - ACHIEVEMENT VARIABLE   115

APPENDIX S. EPPS PSYCHOLOGICAL CHARACTERISTICS CROSS TABULATION - AFFILIATION VARIABLE   116

APPENDIX T. EPPS PSYCHOLOGICAL CHARACTERISTICS CROSS TABULATION - AGGRESSION VARIABLE   117

APPENDIX U. EPPS PSYCHOLOGICAL CHARACTERISTICS CROSS TABULATION - AUTONOMY VARIABLE   118

APPENDIX V. EPPS PSYCHOLOGICAL CHARACTERISTICS CROSS
TABULATION - CHANGE VARIABLE   119

APPENDIX W. EPPS PSYCHOLOGICAL CHARACTERISTICS CROSS
TABULATION - DEFERENCE VARIABLE   120

APPENDIX X. EPPS PSYCHOLOGICAL CHARACTERISTICS CROSS
TABULATION - DOMINANCE VARIABLE   121

APPENDIX Y. EPPS PSYCHOLOGICAL CHARACTERISTICS CROSS
TABULATION - ENDURANCE VARIABLE   122

APPENDIX Z. EPPS PSYCHOLOGICAL CHARACTERISTICS CROSS
TABULATION - EXHIBITION VARIABLE   123

APPENDIX AA. EPPS PSYCHOLOGICAL CHARACTERISTICS CROSS
TABULATION - INTRACEPTION VARIABLE   124

APPENDIX BB. EPPS PSYCHOLOGICAL CHARACTERISTICS CROSS
TABULATION - NURTURANCE VARIABLE   125

APPENDIX CC. EPPS PSYCHOLOGICAL CHARACTERISTICS CROSS
TABULATION - ORDER VARIABLE   126

APPENDIX DD. EPPS PSYCHOLOGICAL CHARACTERISTICS CROSS
TABULATION - SUCCORANCE VARIABLE   127

APPENDIX EE. AVERAGE SCORES OF PSYCHOLOGICAL
CHARACTERISTICS   128

List of Tables

Table 1:   Abasement chi-square test   45

Table 2:   Achievement chi-square test   45

Table 3:   Affiliation chi-square test   45

Table 4:   Aggression chi-square test   46

Table 5:   Autonomy chi-square test   46

Table 6:   Change chi-square test   50

Table 7:   Deference chi-square test   51

Table 8:   Dominance chi-square test   51

Table 9:   Endurance chi-square test   51

Table 10: Exhibition chi-square test   52

Table 11: Intraception chi-square test   52

Table 12: Nurturance chi-square test   52

Table 13: Order chi-square test   53

Table 14: Succorance chi-square test   53

Table 15: Age comparison of both entrepreneur types in reaching success   55

Table 16: Experience of both entrepreneur types in reaching success   56

Table 17: Educational level case summary comparisons   56

Table 18: Number of children chi-square data analysis   64

Table 19: Number of children cross tabulation table   64

Table 20: Waiting period cross tabulation   65

Table 21: Waiting period chi-square test   65

Table 22: Only daughter cross tabulation   67

Table 23: Only daughter chi-square test   67

Table 24: Eldest daughter cross tabulation   68

Table 25: Eldest daughter chi-square test   68

Table 26: Birth theory chi-square test   69

List of Figures

Figure 1: Entrepreneur motivational start up comparison chart   42

Figure 2: Education level case summary   57

Figure 3: Second job comparisons of World Athlete Entrepreneurs and Women
Business Entrepreneurs   59

Figure 4: Second job comparison type   59

Figure 5: Marital status comparison between entrepreneurs   61

CHAPTER 1. INTRODUCTION

Introduction to the Problem

Entrepreneurship continues to interest the general public due to downsizing of corporate businesses (Teal & Carroll, 1999 & Birley, 1989) and lack of long-term security. Additional findings state that individuals who decide to practice this way of life are going against the norms of society. This remains a factor of concern in regards to women. People remain in a psychic prison (Morgan, 1997) when it comes to women in sports and entrepreneurship since the passing of laws for women's rights in the 1970's.

Increasingly, entrepreneurial studies presume business and sports are intertwined and these skills and talents can be transferred to the boardroom. Authoritative researchers conclude entrepreneurship is fulfilling a passion and the professional athlete is utilizing his or her skills and talents to pursue the entrepreneurship road. They are combining what they do best with the entrepreneur prospective in exchange for a paycheck. It is stated that this particular entrepreneurship is part of the entertainment sector.

The sport's industry is huge and rodeo is currently a big player in this field. Barrel racing is a female dominated event in professional rodeo. During this research, it was found that cowgirls are the first female athletes. Robinson (1999) found that cowgirls started pursuing the rodeo trail in the late 1800's to utilize their skills and talents acquired on the ranches. A few impediments, according to history literature, tried to prevent these women from pursuing their venture but they stood firm. Today, cowgirls do have women's rodeos (Women's Professional Rodeo Association) where they participate in a variety of events such as bull riding, bronc riding, roping, and more. Furthermore, they

1

are still allowed to compete with the cowboys in professional rodeos, such as the Professional Rodeo Cowboys Association (PRCA) but it is not the norm, (P. Roberts, personal communication, July 23, 2007). There are and have been women participating in the bronc riding, bull riding, and team roping events.

The cowgirl represents a World Athlete Entrepreneur and she has helped barrel racing to become an industry in itself. Today, while they experience social criticisms, World Athlete Entrepreneurs are accused of not displaying the appropriate entrepreneurship skills. It appears to be a misunderstood environment to society but the barrel racing industry gives the impression to have an opportunity for success if one conducts her business career correctly.

Could the misunderstood appearance be caused by the lack of research? Literature documents the entrepreneurial levels and motives of sport athletes, mostly targeting males. If rodeo cowboys are proven to be entrepreneurs by a 1999 study conducted by Pearson and Haney, what is the difference of a barrel-racing cowgirl?

The purpose of this study is to compare and contrast Woman Barrel Racers with Women Business Entrepreneurs and determine if there are similarities between women who race and women who have their own businesses.

Background

Cowgirls started competing with men in rough stock events in the late 1800's. Studies and literature show successful entrepreneurial motives and performances. During the off-season, they worked second, related jobs as current business entrepreneurs are capable of doing according to literature discussing entrepreneur practices (Robinson,

2

1999). Robinson affirms that these first female athlete activities were more lucrative than many dentists, schoolteachers, and other business professionals in that era.

Barriers emerged trying to prevent these cowgirls from pursuing entrepreneurial endeavors and World War II marked the final turning point that claimed all women were no longer suppose to be associated with the sports industry. This did not stop females. In 1948, the Women's Professional Rodeo Association (WPRA) was organized by a group of determined Texas cowgirls and these women entrepreneurs established policies, strategies, and arbitration skills to help them on their road to success (Robinson, 1999).

Barrel racing is now assumed to be an art. This sports event has become so popular it is an industry of its own and the opportunities are limitless. However, the barrel racing industry is misunderstood, especially in relation to business. Could this be because of the psychic prison explained by Morgan (1997) that society tends to live in? Authoritative studies claim that society has a tendency to get people to believe how it wants them to believe. In addition, it is confirmed that life policies and procedures are practiced because of how society or culture has taught others. This is illustrated by the guidelines passed after World War II claiming women were no longer to be associated with the sports industry or anything outside of the home because it made her less attractive to men for marriage and child-bearing issues (Robinson, 1999).

Statement of the Problem

Studies describe entrepreneurship as a mystifying environment and these authorities portray an entrepreneur as a person who participates in his or her own activity

3

to obtain capital, self-actualization, and achievement by providing his or her own capital to cover the costs, if needed.

Theories are abundantly stated throughout business literature that one has to spend money to make money and a person will not get rich by working for someone else. So, it is claimed, people become nascent entrepreneurs in search for putting their talent levels to use in search of achievement (Danco, 1993). Athletes utilize their sporting capability in pursuit of accomplishing this goal. Extensive research claims business and sports are intertwined in areas of psychological, motivational, and business strategies.

The sports athlete is proven, by authoritative studies and reputable sources, to be an entrepreneur due to the similarity of goals in participating for a) the search of capital, b) self-actualization, and c) achievement. In addition, the sports athlete is related in experiencing the responsibility for his or her own financial resources. Literature synthesizes how other sport athletes practice entrepreneurship strategies. One empirical factor is that most of the literature and studies target males. Pearson and Haney (1999) are among this literature that evaluated and proved rodeo cowboys to be entrepreneurs.

World Athlete Entrepreneurs are criticized for their business motives and these females are denied the proper prestige needed by society and professionals. However, it is speculated this may be due to the lack of educational material or from the psychic prison based on society's expectations of women (Morgan, 1997).

The Purpose

The purpose of this study was to compare and contrast Woman Barrel Racers with Women Business Entrepreneurs and determine if there is an association between women who race and women who have their own businesses.

The objectives of this study are:

1. Compare and contrast the components that define successful Woman Business Entrepreneurs and World Athlete Entrepreneurs.

2. Compare and contrast the psychological and motivational factors found among Women Business Entrepreneurs and World Athlete Entrepreneurs.

3. Compare and contrast the strategical business functions practiced in the pursuit of success by Woman Business Entrepreneurs and World Athlete Entrepreneurs (e.g. financing, benchmarking, types of capital, advertising, sponsorship).

4. Compare and contrast the impediments experienced by Women Business Entrepreneurs and World Athlete Entrepreneurs.

5. Compare Women Business Entrepreneurs and World Athlete Entrepreneurs with the Birth Theory and the Only or Eldest Daughter Syndrome.

Rationale

Current research studies intermingle sports athlete entrepreneurs with business entrepreneurs in the objectives stated above. This includes the psychological, motivational, and business aspects. There are numerous reasons for the importance of proving the similarities between women who race and women who have their own businesses. They are to (a) enhance cultural education and prevent further criticisms, (b) to educate World Athlete Entrepreneurs, (c) help the World Athlete Entrepreneur build a business strategy, and (d) to educate business owners and corporations about this environment; in hopes, of presenting a positive clarification about this growing industry. Additionally, it is possible, by providing this knowledge, corporations and individual decision-makers will receive a positive reaction about the business tactics of World Athlete Entrepreneurs and increase decision-making authority for sponsorship and endorsement decisions. Additional research discusses the fact that the sports athlete entrepreneur depends on sponsors to help with finances so he or she can pursue what is done best. This appears to be a logical interpretation similar to business entrepreneurs who seek advertisers.

The findings of this study create new knowledge of various business aspects of the sport. Many World Athlete Entrepreneurs strive for professionalism and to make this a business career.

Research Questions

1. Are Women Business Entrepreneurs and World Athlete Entrepreneurs successful?

2. How do Women Business Entrepreneurs and World Athlete Entrepreneurs measure success?

3. What are the psychological and motivational traits shared by World Athlete Entrepreneurs and Woman Business Entrepreneurs?

4. What human and social capital factors do World Athlete Entrepreneurs and Women Business Entrepreneurs attain (e.g. age, experience, education)?

5. What kinds of financial availability do World Athlete Entrepreneurs use during their venture?

6. Are both Women Entrepreneurs employed in other disciplines for additional financing?

7. How do World Athlete Entrepreneurs and Women Business Entrepreneurs practice the strategic art of benchmarking?

8. Do Women Business Entrepreneurs and World Athlete Entrepreneurs experience the same barriers of (a) financial issues, (b) family, and (c) genetic stereotyping.

9. Do World Athlete Entrepreneurs and Women Business Entrepreneurs share in the same Birth Theory or Only/Eldest Daughter Syndrome?

Significance of the Study

This exploratory, comparative, case study investigates what and how the two entrepreneurs being studied are associated. Numerous studies prove sports athletes to be connected with business and entrepreneurship; however, most of the studies analyzed elaborate on males.

No studies are conducted in the area of barrel racers linking to entrepreneurship. To the researcher's knowledge this subject is being evaluated, observed, and analyzed for the first time. The research study gives the potential to create a social change and a better understanding of this industry. It gives an accurate illustration of the definition of an entrepreneur given in the definition of terms and confirms the entrepreneurial motives of World Athlete Entrepreneurs.

This research study evaluates, compares, and contrasts the business strategies of World Athlete Entrepreneurs and Women Business Entrepreneurs.

Definition of Terms

Abasement. To feel guilty when one does something wrong, to accept blame when things do not go right; to feel that personal pain and misery suffered does more good than harm, to feel the need for punishment for wrong doing, to feel better when giving in and avoiding a fight than when having one's own way. To feel depressed by the inability to handle situations, to feel timid in the presence of superiors, to feel inferior to others in most respects.

Accounts Receivable. Money owed by clients.

Achievement. To do one's best, to be successful, to accomplish tasks requiring skill and effort, to be a recognized authority, to accomplish something of great significance. To be able to do things better than others. To write a great novel or play.

Affiliation. To be loyal to friends, to participate in friendly groups, to do things for friends, to form new friendships, to make as many friends as possible, to share things with friends; to do things with friends rather than alone; to form strong attachments.

Aggression. To attack contrary points of view, to tell others what one thinks about them, to criticize others publicly, to make fun of others, to tell others off when disagreeing with them, to get revenge for insults, to become angry, to blame others when things go wrong, to read newspaper accounts of violence.

Autonomy. Independent action of an individual in bringing forward an idea and carrying it through until the finish. Self-direction. To be able to come and go as desired. To be independent of others in making decisions.

Benchmarking. A business strategy allowing for the observation of other competition in which, the objective is to identify the best practices in performing an activity in order to stay to stay up with the competition and gain better results.

Birth Theory. One who is from a family with similar background. For analysis of this research study, in regards to World Athlete Entrepreneurs, it pertains to families with a rodeo background or involvement in the horse industry. For a Women Business Entrepreneur, it pertains to one who is from a family who owns or has owned a business.

Bootstrapping. Funds heavily relied on from internally generated retained earnings, leasing equipment, customer advances, second mortgages, and use of credit cards. The use of personal and other generated funds to support business activity.

Business Angels. A wealthy individual willing to invest personal money into a business with growth potential.

Change. To do new and different things, to travel, to meet new people, to experience novelty and change in daily routine; to experiment and to try new things; to eat in new and different places; to try new and different jobs; to move about the country and live in different places; to participate in new fads and fashions.

Cultural Meaning Transfer Theory. A theory that proposes that meanings are inspired through the purchase of good and services, in addition, to the product themselves.

Deference. To get suggestions from others, to find out what others think, to follow instructions and do what is expected, to praise others, to tell others that they have done a good job, to accept the leadership of others, to read about great men, to conform to custom and avoid the unconventional, to let others make decisions.

Dominance. The need to influence others; to be a leader in groups to which one belongs, to be regarded by others as a leader; to persuade and influence others to do what one wants; to supervise and direct the actions of others.

Endorsement. A marketing tool that utilizes athletes to represent a company's product or service.

Endurance. Commitment until a job is finished; work hard at a task; stay up late working in order to get a job done; to put in long hours of work without distraction.

Entrepreneur. A person who participates in his or her own activity to obtain capital, self-actualization, and achievement. He or she is responsible for her own financial resources to pay for business expenses in order to continue the venture.

Environmental hostility. Reflects the fierceness of competition, discourages new formation of ventures.

Exhibition - To say witty and clever things, to tell amusing jokes and stories, to talk about personal adventures and experiences, to have others notice and comment upon one's appearance, to say things just to see what effect it will have on others, to talk about personal achievements, to be the center of attention, to use words that others do not know the meaning of, to ask questions others cannot answer.

Human Capital. Knowledge, age, education, skills, and experience.

Intraception. The need to analyze one's motives and feelings, to observe others, to understand how others feel about problems, to put one's self in another's place, to judge people by why they do things rather than by what they do, to analyze the behavior of others, to analyze the motives of others, to predict how others will act.

Micro-lenders. People who make small loans to emerging companies.

Nascent entrepreneur. A person who undertakes activities to create a business.

Nurturance. To help friends when they are in trouble, to assist others less fortunate, to treat others with kindness and sympathy, to forgive others, to do small favors for others, to be generous with others, to sympathize with others who are hurt or sick, to show a great deal of affection toward others, to have others confide in one about personal problems.

Order. To have written work neat and organized, to make plans before starting on a difficult task, to have things organized, to keep things neat and orderly, to make advance plans when taking a trip, to organize details of work, to keep letters and files according to some system, to have meals organized and a definite time for eating, to have things arranged so that they run smoothly without change.

Social Capital. Actual and potential resources individuals obtain from knowing others, being part of a network, or from being known and having a good reputation.

Sports Athlete. One participating in different sporting events (e.g. football, tennis, golf, and other equestrian events).

Succorance. To have others provide help when in trouble, to seek encouragement from others, to have others be kindly, to have others be sympathetic and understanding about personal problems, to receive a great deal of affection from others, to have others do favors cheerfully, to be helped by others when depressed, to have others feel sorry when one is sick, to have a fuss made over one when hurt.

World Athlete. The barrel-racing cowgirl.

Assumptions and Limitations

According to studies, sports and business are connected and research studies give positive results regarding sport athletes sharing the same psychological and motivational features as a business entrepreneur. Therefore, World Athlete Entrepreneurs are assumed to share in this philosophy. Personality tests are assumed to be appropriate measures to use as a valid and reliable methodology for collecting the psychological data in this study.

It is assumed there are few differences in the business factors that relate World Athletes to Women Business Entrepreneurs. Financial resources are the World Athlete Entrepreneur's responsibility and it appears they rely on the same capital factors as Women Business Entrepreneurs. The data collection and analysis of both types of entrepreneurs will prove whether similarities in entrepreneurial business motives of the World Athlete Entrepreneur exist.

The World Athlete Entrepreneur seems committed to business motives and continues striving for self-promotion. This study evaluates World Athlete Entrepreneurs by (a) analyzing their psychological, motivational, and strategical motives and (b) synthesizing the results to compare and contrast factors in finding a relationship with Women Business Entrepreneurs. The results will not only help World Athlete Entrepreneurs pursue their goal but also help society, business professionals, and decision makers to be open minded to this industry.

The goal of this research study is to prove similarities between both entrepreneurs; however, it is assumed that gender stereotyping and the closed mindedness of society will still give limitations in development of positive attitudes about this environment.

Nature of the Study

To find the relationship between the two research topics a mixed-method design study was implemented to gather the data for analysis. An Ethnographic methodology was used to attain the data; in which, case studies were developed. The Edwards Personal Preference Schedule (Edwards, 1953) calculated the data to investigate the psychological and motivational characteristics. Permission to use this test was granted by David Edwards, trustee of the estate of author, Allen L. Edwards. The Ethnographic methodology was utilized to seek the understanding of cultural meanings that people use to organize and interpret their experiences as explained by other studies and documentaries. The barrel-racing environment is a misunderstood culture that society

11

remains poorly informed. Creswell (1998) advises that using a qualitative perception to this environment presents a detailed view and portrays a holistic picture to enable the reading audience to be more acceptable to the outcome. This study also implements a quantitative nature of information to intensify the relationship among variables (2002) in order to broaden the minds of readers who need statistical data analysis for belief confirmation.

The data was collected by observations, surveys, and questionnaires. Observations were made by (a) getting to personally know more of the people in the barrel racing environment, (b) share communication, (c) personal experience, and (d) observing habits and preferences.

Organization of the Remainder of the Study

Chapter 2 discusses the appropriate literature that gives a foundation of characteristics and other business strategic motives to compare World Athlete Entrepreneurs and Women Business Entrepreneurs. Chapter 3 discusses the past and present methodological procedures used in relation to this investigation. Chapter 4 portrays and analyzes the data gathered from the data instruments. Chapter 5 reports the final results found from the investigation of chapter 4 data and recommends additional research ideas.

CHAPTER 2. LITERATURE REVIEW

Introduction

The literature review brought to focus many aspects of the entrepreneurial

practices and factors experienced by both businesswomen and sports athletes. To

compare and contrast Women Business Entrepreneurs and World Athlete Entrepreneurs

the need to get a concentration of what constitutes a female entrepreneur was

investigated. To get an accurate analysis of comparing Women Business Entrepreneurs

and World Athlete Entrepreneurs an assessment of (a) psychological and motivational

factors, (b) business strategies, (c) birth theory, d) barriers, and (e) Only or Eldest

Daughter Syndrome was investigated to get a foundation of characteristics pertaining to

Woman Business Entrepreneurs. The (a) distinguishment of psychological and

motivational characteristics, and (b) defining the different business strategies of how

these Women Business Entrepreneurs maneuver their endeavors was important in

explaining the motives of World Athlete Entrepreneurs and how they stay successful.

There are research studies in different areas of entrepreneurship. During the

investigation of these studies, some authors claim there are research studies not valid or

reliable due to the definition of the entrepreneur used for that particular research (Woldt,

2005). These authors claim this prevents other studies to utilize them as relational

literature reviews. However, observation confronted these definitions and found the same

frequently used words in the context that makes it practical to get a valid and reliable

result. One study defines an entrepreneur to be a person conducting an activity to create wealth and profit (e.g. Blanchflower & Oswald, 1998) and other study definitions have included the words, for self-actualization and achievement. Further, it is explained that it is up to this person to find the resources to continue their endeavors.

A research study pertaining to areas of sports (e.g. Hunter and Mayo, 1999) claim a sport is about business and sports management and it is an applied science moving into the norm. Other researchers claim that sports and business are intertwined and professional athletes, whether team involved or individually oriented, conduct business affairs like a business entrepreneur. Thompson (1999) backs this theory and states entrepreneurs are everywhere, including sports. He gives an example in his study of yacht racers who possess and conduct activities as an entrepreneur. The results show the sharing of psychological factors in having clear visions of their pursuit. They are motivated, determined, and responsible for their own financing to get their job done.

Most studies are more concerned with men entrepreneurs and discuss the areas of (a) strategies, (b) psychological and motivational issues, and (c) financing. It was not until the 1970's when Bruni, Gherardi, and Poggio (2004) claim women entrepreneurs were finally acknowledged and therefore, research studies regarding women entrepreneurs, started in the 1980's. Since then, Hormozi (2004) states female entrepreneurs are no longer outcasts and are associated with innovation and honor. This theory can be debated after reading studies expressing impediments, such as gender stereotyping, experienced by Women Business Entrepreneurs in today's society. Women athletes are more common today, whether it is recreational or professional. The World Athlete Entrepreneur still experiences stereotyping among culture and professional elites.

Entrepreneur Barriers

Societal culture is one main impediment that still lingers, even though there are laws for women's rights and other women's issues. Morgan (1997) expresses that people get others to believe or do what they want them to. Stereotyping is still a heavy influence and it projects beliefs and perceptions of a theory that women are lacking characteristics needed for successful entrepreneurship and they are less successful (Catley & Hamilton, 1998). Catley and Hamilton discusses that this theory is incorrect according to a 1991 research study by Kalleberg and Leicht.

Other research studies conclude additional impediments faced by female entrepreneurs. These include financial concerns such as (a) lack of capital, (b) no guaranteed income, (c) losing savings, (d) understanding tax issues, and (e) bookkeeping issues. Other concerns are (f) the ability to get started, (g) networks, (h) location, (i) getting the appropriate clientele, and (j) competition. However, three barriers are consistently experienced, according to past studies, (a) financial issues, (b) family issues, such as responsibility of children and spousal support, and (c) gender stereotyping (Catley & Hamilton, 1997; Blanchflower & Oswald, 1998; Morris, Miyasaki, Walters, & Coombes, 2006; Hatala, 2005; Beugelsdijk & Noorderhaven, 2005; Skelton, 2006; and Winn, 2004). Do World-Athlete Entrepreneurs experience these same three impediments?

One particular concern for Women Business Entrepreneurs is family. Authoritative studies analyzed the effects of family responsibilities. Brodsky finds that Women Business Entrepreneurs were most likely to be divorced (1993). Considerations of the reasons why were of concern. An article analyzed about men business

15

entrepreneurs stated wives had to be cooperative with them. The literature claimed females married to men business entrepreneurs must be patient. Is gender stereotyping coming into vision? Are men considered uncooperative with wives in this field? Experience shows that this can be likely but it is still considered an assumption. Bruni, Gherardi, and Poggio's study discusses the socio-culture issue in this area and it is believed that the primary role of women is family and domestic responsibility. Therefore, it reduces the credibility of women's intent on setting up businesses in a variety of ways. There are supportive, authoritative researchers that proved Women Business Entrepreneurs to show the opposite and demonstrate a compulsion necessary for starting a business and endow women to see it as an opportunity (2004).

Experience with World Athlete Entrepreneurs proved the long hours of travel, practice, and other competing functions (such as paying expenses) needed. Does this prevent the World Athlete Entrepreneur to experience the same family impediment or concern?

It is shown female entrepreneurs are still frowned upon in certain areas, especially in the rodeo field. Barrel racing has climbed to the top of favorite events in the rodeo circuit and it has become an industry of its own. But, it is still misunderstood by culture and business professionals.

Pearson and Haney (1999) conducted a particular study of interest. However, this study relates to the discussion earlier of many entrepreneurial studies targeting males. Their ethnographic study confirmed cowboys to be entrepreneurs. This qualitative study interviewed cowboys using semi-structured and structured questions. Observations and interviews were conducted with various parties involved with rodeo. The objectives were stated within the literature to confirm the entrepreneurial level of the cowboy but the exact questions asked were not stated. The results of the investigation concluded that the cowboy fits with certain entrepreneur traits such as domestic problems in regards to financial resources, family, and education.

The entrepreneur definition used in the Pearson and Haney (1999) study expresses it as one who organizes and manages a commercial endeavor that usually involves financial risks. Positive confirmation of relation to the entrepreneur definition was concluded by facts of cowboys having travel expenses, holding second jobs, and paying entry fees. They also experience the same strategic practices of an entrepreneur because it is up to the cowboy how his endeavor continues.

Past Research. Pearson and Haney's study is similar to this current study but it only concentrates on the basic levels of entrepreneurship. The current study being analyzed investigates specific factors and collects data from the actual World Athlete Entrepreneurs. Pearson and Haney's study confirms their data was collected from an estimated 27 subjects which, included cowboys, rodeo producers, stock contractors, and other forms of personnel involved with rodeo and retrieved the basic information to determine the entrepreneurship levels. This starts an excellent foundation but the reliability and validity is of concern. It is assumed a greater number of the competing cowboys need to be analyzed in this investigation to get a more specific conclusion of entrepreneur practices. According to R. Lamm (personal communication, 2006) and other authoritative resources, a minimum of thirty subjects is needed for a reliable and valid measurement.

How do these athletes survive and become successful? The basic knowledge recited in the past study is helpful in understanding entrepreneurial motives; however, this particular investigation condenses the participants to actual World Athlete Entrepreneurs and an analysis of the strategic practices are more involved.

Entrepreneur Success

Sage (1993) claims there is no formula that exists for creating successful entrepreneurs but Danco (1993) claims nascent entrepreneurs needed certain qualities in order to pursue his or her startup. Nascent entrepreneurs must have (a) a long-range point of view, (b) be flexible to redefine business areas that need to be focused on as the venture grows, and (c) have a supportive family. One important trait continually stressed in defining a successful entrepreneur is that their work is their passion and not a job (Garret, 2006). The World-Athlete Entrepreneur has a passion for what she is doing and continues to strive for the entrepreneurial goal of success.

Entrepreneurs want their passion to become successful. What specific elements contribute to the term successful? Sage (1993) declares there is no definite formula for success but, the current literature discloses that to become successful, an entrepreneur must develop or possess quality traits such as (a) integrity, (b) initiative, (c) commitment, (d) drive and determination, (e) confidence, (f) self-direction, (g) salesmanship, (h) leadership, and (i) persistence (Garret, 2006). Business success varies between entrepreneurs by what their goals are. Danco (1993) explains that a founder's true success is in the continuity of the business or activity. Yet, other researchers find that success is defined in the (a) profit, (b) growth in sales, (c) employees, (d) size, (e) satisfaction, or (f) other financial performances such as stakeholders (Woldt, 2005). Everyone has his or her

18

own definition. How does the World Athlete Entrepreneur's definition of success fit in relation to a Woman Business Entrepreneur?

Entrepreneur Psychological and Motivation Characteristics

Entrepreneurs are further acknowledged to have the same common psychological characteristics and motivational factors proving to be beneficial in the success of entrepreneurship. Studies have used several types of personality tests to arrive at this conclusion. The same psychological and motivational factors have appeared among entrepreneurs in studies and, according to VanGilderen, Thurik, and Bosma (2005), these are important in predicting a business start up. Common characteristics are (a) high need for achievement, (b) autonomy, (c) change, (d) dominance, (e) growth, (f) optimism, (g) creativity, (h) high energy levels, (i) locus of control, (j) risk-taking, (k) energy and social adroitness, (l) preference for earning through action and experimentation, (m) a preference for intuition and thinking, (n) hard work, (o) nurturing, (p) responsibility, (q) acceptance, (r) reward, (s) orientation, (t) optimism, and (u) organization (e.g. Catley & Hamilton, 1998; Brodsky, 1993; Caird, 1993; Hormozi, 2004; and Llewellyn & Wilson, 2003.). Authoritative researchers find these characteristics are related with sport athlete entrepreneurs.

Arguments are found throughout the literature review whether entrepreneurs are the world's largest risk takers. McFarland (2005) debates this risk taking characteristic and claims it as a myth. The results of his study placed entrepreneurs on the 83rd percentile for this category. This is a high score but, according to this researcher, these scores are usually found among top athletes and elite military units. Therefore, this conclusion confirmed the assumption that entrepreneurs and athletes are compatible in this specific psychological area.

Occupational flexibility is found to be an attractive factor for supplemental income (Bruni, Gherardi, & Poggio, 2004). It adds to the additional motivators in entrepreneurship and, according to Morris, Miyaski, & Walters (2006), other motivators were expressed as the ability for equilibrium between economic goals and noneconomic goals.

Self-talk was another similar psychological and motivational factor found among athletes and entrepreneurs (Neck, Neck, Manz, & Godwin, 1999). Both entrepreneurs must believe in his or her capabilities to initiate and complete functions through his or her own actions (Virtanen, nd).

Further analysis of entrepreneurship motivators find Robinson's reason for cowgirls getting on the rodeo trail is in exact relation to Catley and Hamilton's (1998) confirmation that women start businesses to be able to use a skill or talent. Their suggestion of work matching a person gives a person a sense of meaning and affects the type of work performed.

Women Business Entrepreneur Strategy

Strategic plans experienced by Women Business Entrepreneurs are in the areas of financing their venture, benchmarking, and types of capital needed. The type of capital one possesses appears to be of special importance.

Human capital. Social capital is found to play a significant role in entrepreneurial success. Baron and Markman (2000) claim having cooperation of others and a significant amount of network projects greater financial outcomes. Madsen, Neergaard, and Ulhoi

20

(2003) investigated human capital and relate it to characteristics of (a) positive judgment, (b) insight, (c) creativity, (d) vision, and (e) intelligence. Catley and Hamilton (1998) found women business entrepreneurs to be better educated than men business entrepreneurs and that age is a positive influence for success. These two researchers find the average age of successful businesswomen to be 35 years of age or older. It is assumed by experience that the successful World Athlete Entrepreneur is in this same age range.

Finance. Authoritative figures claim that Women Business Entrepreneurs find it hard to finance a venture. However, research performed by Buttner and Rosen (1989); Catley and Hamilton (1998); and Carter, Brush, Greene, Gatewood, and Hart (2002) find no evidence of female discrimination in lending practices in the United States. But, according to the study of Carter, et al. women are required to provide higher levels of collateral making it hard for her to proceed with getting loans.

Due to this circumstance, Women Business Entrepreneurs have to find financing in other places. Studies find that Women Business Entrepreneurs rely more on personal savings but also look toward (a) micro-lenders, (b) business angels, and (c) account receivables (Kom, 2005). MasterCard conducted a research study that concluded 64% of small business owners use plastic for business expenses and 57% use personal or small business cards (de Paula, 2003). Bootstrapping is another area practiced and described by Carter, Brush, Greene, Gatewood, and Hart (2002). This practice is effectively seen in business growth and builds on personal equity and debt (2002). Observation of various documents claim sports athletes experience many financial strategies in relation to business professionals. Does the World Athlete Entrepreneur have the availability of finding appropriate financing and what kind of financing is relied on? Can it be assumed

21

World Athlete Entrepreneurs rely on bootstrapping for financing their venture? Does this give an accurate relation to Women Business Entrepreneurs?

Past research of financing examples. Pearson and Haney's (1999) study confirmed cowboy entrepreneurs practice the same strategic business motives because it is up to him whether his endeavor continues. Women Business Entrepreneurs strategize business motives in the continuation of their venture. So, why would it be different for World Athlete Entrepreneurs? The appearance of this answer seems conclusive that it is not. Gray (2004) illustrated the business strategies and motivation of World Athlete Entrepreneurs with Kelly Kaminski, world-champion barrel racer. In the beginning, she barrel raced on the weekends and taught elementary school during the week. After reaching her financial goal, she quit her teaching job to go full time racing. For her 2004 year, between (a) winnings, (b) endorsements, and (c) training/breeding services, she grossed $202,000. Her direct expenses amounted to $34,000 and left her a net profit of $168,000. Her truck was won by an organizational sponsorship provided by Dodge and another sponsor supplied her with a luxury RV/trailer.

To support additional literature of entrepreneurial practices of World Athlete Entrepreneurs, the researcher conducted an interview for an article to be placed in her publication with Charmayne James (2004), eleven-time world barrel racing champion. It was acknowledged that Charmayne began her entrepreneurial endeavors at a very young age. Her parents were business entrepreneurs and they raised her the same way having to pay for her own competing expenses. At the young age of 13, she won her first world championship and, now in her early thirties, she is currently known as the million-dollar cowgirl.

Additional financing opportunities. Advertising, sponsorships, and endorsements play a significant part in both ventures. They are interrelated because each one appears to be a part of the other. These strategies give a cultural meaning transfer theory on a product or service. Endorsements and sponsorships add additional reputation to a product or service. Endorsements have been around for as long as advertising has existed according to Daneshvary and Schwer (2000). It is a marketing tool that uses athletes to represent products (Mittelstaedt, Riesz, & Burns, 2000). Companies are required to look at the cultural meaning transfer theory and be selective in who they endorse. The effectiveness depends on the match between the endorser and the product. Endorsements are said to be a risk factor depending on the credibility and professionalism of the athlete according to Crompton (2004). Negative influence of an athlete can be detrimental to a product according to Erdogan, Baker, and Tagg (2004) and, therefore, this athlete entrepreneur must present and conduct behavior accordingly.

Sponsorships are advantageous for a company and it provides an effective communications tool that alters and enhances a company's image and reputation (Hickman, Lawrence, & Ward 2004). Sponsorships are similar to endorsements. Kelly Kaminski (world champion World Athlete Entrepreneur) has commented (P. Roberts, personal communication, June 2005) that her venture is not possible without her sponsors.

Benchmarking. The final strategic process analyzed is benchmarking. Throughout business literature and documentation, it is stated that this management tool is excellent for identifying better performance capabilities. Benchmarking functions include (a) observing how others perform, (b) collecting the data, and (c) analyzing it to compare its

23

business strategies, in order, to become more competitive. The data results offer an opportunity for learning new ideas, creativity, and innovation according to Parker and Kovacs (2001).

Pearson and Haney described the cowboy entrepreneur's benchmarking practice. Cowboys claim that winning and breaking records are viewed as benchmarks and signs of improvement (1999). This benchmarking practice is of concern because winning and breaking records along with signs of improvement is a means of benchmarking but it is only analyzing personal achievement. The current researcher's knowledge about benchmarking is an observing, collecting data, and analyzing practices of other competition to find better procedures on reaching success? How are cowboys measuring the competition to gain better results? Pearson and Haney's study also develops concern in regards to what is analyzed and how they are incorporated with what the specific cowboy is doing to reach their success goal? The participants in Pearson and Haney's study ranged from the cowboy, to stock contractors, and other behind the scenes personnel.

Observation and personal experience projects World Athlete Entrepreneurs network amongst each other on equipment, training methods, horse nutrition, and other factors for their benchmarking practices. The current study analyzes this practice and confirms whether these are accurate factors in the benchmarking procedures. Furthermore, the analysis deals specifically with World Athlete Entrepreneurs.

Entrepreneur Genetic Theories

Studies debate the genetic theories of entrepreneurship. Some researchers argue whether entrepreneurs are born with entrepreneurial traits or taught. Studies suggest

24

successful entrepreneurs are from families with an entrepreneurial background, which is known as the birth theory (deVries & Kets, 1996; Morris, Miyasaki, Walters, & Coombes, 2006; Anonymous, 1995). Additional studies claim Women Business Entrepreneurs are only or eldest daughters. Are successful World Athlete Entrepreneurs similar to these theories?

The literature review provides a great foundation in proceeding with the current research study. It gives a concentration of data to analyze in comparing and contrasting World Athlete Entrepreneurs with Women Business Entrepreneurs to determine if there is an association between women who race and women who have their own businesses.

CHAPTER 3. METHODOLOGY

The purpose of this study was to compare and contrast World Athlete Entrepreneurs with Women Business Entrepreneurs and determine if there is an association between women who race and women who have their own businesses. Nine questions were asked to find the association of these two groups:

1. Are Women Business Entrepreneurs and World Athlete Entrepreneurs successful?

2. How do Women Business Entrepreneurs and World Athlete Entrepreneurs measure success?

3. What are the psychological and motivational traits shared by World Athlete Entrepreneurs and Woman Business Entrepreneurs?

4. What human and social capital factors do World Athlete Entrepreneurs and Women Business Entrepreneurs attain (e.g. age, experience, education)?

5. What kinds of financial availability do World Athlete Entrepreneurs use during their venture?

6. Are both women entrepreneurs employed in other disciplines for additional financing?

7. How do World Athlete Entrepreneurs and Women Business Entrepreneurs practice the strategic art of benchmarking?

8. Do Women Business Entrepreneurs and World Athlete Entrepreneurs experience the same barriers of (a) financial issues, (b) family, and (c) genetic stereotyping.

9. Do World Athlete Entrepreneurs and Women Business Entrepreneurs share in the same Birth Theory or Only/Eldest Daughter Syndrome?

A mixed-method design was implemented to analyze and answer these research questions. Case studies developed by an Ethnographic methodology collected the data. The Edwards Personal Preference Schedule collected the data to investigate the

26

psychological and motivational characteristics. The Ethnographic methodology exploited the understanding of the cultural meanings people use to organize and interpret their experiences in the barrel-racing environment (Tellis, 1997). The barrel racing environment is a misunderstood culture that society remains poorly informed about. Observations and questionnaires collected additional data.

Design of the Study

This exploratory, comparative, and ethnographic research study utilizes case studies because of the many elements involved in the barrel-racing industry. This culture remains misunderstood and issues are buried below the surface of current awareness (Shank & Villela, 2004). Tellis (1997) explains case study methodology is applicable for usage in an empirical investigation within real life context. The qualitative research portion of this study (a) allowed for interaction with participants (Creswell, 1994) being studied and (b) portrayed a detailed view and holistic picture (Creswell, 1998).

The current study frame of questions asking who, what, where, how, and why, determined the case study to be a relevant strategy to use in this investigation according to Tellis (1997) and Sorheim (2005).

The exploratory design of the study measures the *what* questions listed below by their specific research question number stated in the previous section:

3. What are the psychological and motivational traits shared by both entrepreneurs?

4. What human and social factors do successful World Athlete and Women Business Entrepreneurs attain?

5. What kinds of financial availability do World Athlete Entrepreneurs and Women Business Entrepreneurs use during their venture?

27

8. What same barriers do World Athlete Entrepreneurs and Women Business Entrepreneurs experience?

9. What are the genetic similarities between World Athlete Entrepreneurs and Women Business Entrepreneurs?

The explanatory design of the study answers the *how* questions listed below by the specific research question number stated in the previous section:

2. How do Women Business Entrepreneurs and World Athlete Entrepreneurs measure success?

6. How do both women entrepreneurs gain additional financing?

7. How does the World Athlete Entrepreneur and the Women Business Entrepreneur practice the strategic art of benchmarking?

This present perspective case study investigated psychological and motivational characteristics and the business strategies of Women Business Entrepreneurs and World Athlete Entrepreneurs. It retrieved data from participants by observations, surveys, and questionnaires in order to investigate the descriptions and interpretations of the data.

Quantitative analysis is implemented to form a mixed-method research study. This form of analysis confirms the relationship of variables (Creswell, 2002). Furthermore, as explained by Creswell (1998), the implementation of a mixed method procedure helped in constructing validity usage in determining the significance of the study.

To help in this research study a publication was developed by the researcher in the state of Florida in 2004. This publication, called the Florida Equine Athlete, is targeted for the barrel racers in the state of Florida and is now on its third year of distribution. As Shank and Villella (2004) illustrate, it has developed a form of partnership with the

28

researcher and World Athlete Entrepreneurs. This tremendously helped the researcher become more involved with the barrel racing industry participants.

The Edward's Personal Preference Schedule collected the data needed for question number 2. This test investigates fifteen psychological and motivational characteristics. However, for this particular study, fourteen of the characteristics were analyzed to find the psychological and motivational characteristics shared by World Athlete Entrepreneurs and Women Business Entrepreneurs. The fourteen characteristic variables analyzed were (a) achievement, (b) deference, (c) order, (d) exhibition, (e) autonomy, (f) affiliation, (g) intraception, (h) succorance, (i) dominance, (j) abasement, (k) nurturance, (l) change, (m) endurance, and (n) aggression. The definitions of the characteristics are found in chapter 1 in the definition of terms.

The Statistical Package for the Social Science (2000), SPSS, analyzed the data for research questions number 3, 5, 8, and 9, respectively, to develop results and create conclusions.

Population and Sample

This study targeted a total population of sixty participants which, consisted of a minimum sample in each category (a) thirty World Athlete Entrepreneurs and (b) thirty Women Business Entrepreneurs. Selective sampling was used in finding participants as each participant had to meet requirements in order to be eligible for this study (Appendix D). Each entrepreneur had to (a) be between 18-75 years of age and (b) produce a gross profit. Additional requirements were (a) World Athlete Entrepreneurs had to participate in at least forty rodeos or barrel racing events a year and (b) Woman Business Entrepreneurs must have owned her own business for at least one year. The population of

29

thirty for each entrepreneur category makes the study valid and reliable (R. Lamm, personal communication, July 2006).

Email and telephone communication was the main source of finding research participants. Posting on the Florida Equine Athlete website was an additional source of advertisement. The geographic locations of World Athlete Entrepreneur participants were Florida, Texas, Arizona, Oklahoma, Colorado, Kentucky, and California. The Women Business Entrepreneur participants were found in Florida, Alaska, New York, Pennsylvania, Ohio, Georgia, Maine, and Massachusetts.

Instrumentation

The employment of questionnaires, using structured and unstructured questions collected the data to analyze all questions (Appendix A and B) except for question number 2. The Edwards Personal Preference Schedule (EPPS) investigated the characteristics of the psychological and motivational traits of both types of entrepreneurs. David Edwards, the trustee of the estate of author, Allen L. Edwards, gave permission to use the EPPS. This research study analyzed fourteen of the fifteen psychological and motivational characteristics offered by the EPPS in order to find a relationship of the two independent variables (a) World Athlete Entrepreneur and (b) Women Business Entrepreneur.

Data Collection

The collection of primary data was gathered to acquire an understanding of the association between World Athlete Entrepreneurs and Women Business Entrepreneurs.

30

This case study developed an explanatory-exploratory design of questions listed at the beginning of this chapter that investigated *what* and *how* (Tellis, 1997) of the two population samples.

Data was gathered by (a) a questionnaire developed by the researcher consisting of structured and unstructured questions (Appendix A and B) and (b) a survey called the Edwards Personal Preference Schedule. Selective sampling was employed in seeking specific World Athlete Entrepreneurs and Women Business Entrepreneurs in order to provide a measurement that would confirm an accurate result.

Data Analysis

This study concentrated mostly on exploiting questionnaires with the use of structured and unstructured questions to find the (a) human and financial capital, (b) business strategies practiced, (c) additional jobs performed, (d) benchmarking practices, (e) birth theory, (f) eldest/only daughter syndrome, and (g) success factors of World Athlete Entrepreneurs and Women Business Entrepreneurs. Excellent foundations of characteristics are repetitively found in the literature review. These research studies commonly used self designed questionnaires and in-depth interviews to investigate and collect data (e.g. Morris, Miyasaki, Walters, & Coombes, 2006; Sorheim, 2005; Madsen, Neergaard, & Ulhoi, 2003; and Pearson & Haney, 1999). This accumulated data gave a concrete foundation of principles to compare relationships and contrast distinguishment to receive a reliable and valid result.

The Edwards Personal Preference Schedule was employed to investigate related psychological and motivation characteristics between the two independent variables. This is a qualitative test and according to Caird (1993), it is an objective, reasonable, and reliable personality test. The subject ranks the importance of needs in order of individual priorities. Common characteristics of business entrepreneurs, found in other research, include (a) needing high achievement, (b) autonomy, (c) change, (d) dominance, (e) growth, (f) optimism, (g) creativity, (h) high energy levels, (i) locus of control, (j) risk-taking, (k) energy and social adroitness, (l) preference for earning through action and experimentation, (m) a preference for intuition and thinking, (n) hard work, (o) nurturing, (p) responsibility, (q) acceptance, (r) reward orientation, (s) optimism, and (t) organization (e.g. Catley & Hamilton, 1998; Brodsky, 1993; Caird, 1993; Hormozi, 2004; and Llewellyn & Wilson, 2003.). However, these studies are frequently men oriented or of unknown gender. Therefore, it is assumed these characteristics are of a different nature for Women Business Entrepreneurs. Various types of personality tests were used in other research but this study utilized the Edwards Personal Preference Schedule (EPPS) and was given to both World Athlete Entrepreneurs and Women Business Entrepreneurs. Providing the same questions to both participant types increased the validity of this investigation. Analysis of the data collected by the EPPS was carried out using the Statistical Package for the Social Sciences (2000).

Many impediments are found in the literature review that tries to prevent Women Business Entrepreneurs from succeeding. These factors include (a) lack of capital, (b) no guaranteed income, (c) losing savings, (d) understanding tax issues, (e) bookkeeping issues, (f) ability to get started, (g) networks, (h) location, (i) getting the appropriate clientele, and (j) competition. However, the three common barriers consistently making a presence for Women Business Entrepreneurs were (a) financial ability, (b) family, and (c)

32

gender stereotyping (Catley & Hamilton, 1997; Blanchflower & Oswald, 1998; Morris, Miyasaki, Walters, & Coombes, 2006; Hatala, 2005; Beugelsdijk & Noorderhaven, 2005; Skelton, 2006; and Winn, 2004). The questionnaires developed for this study examined these three barriers with both entrepreneur types.

Ethical Considerations

Protection of Human Participants

Participants joining in this study were treated in an ethical manner. There were no foreseen risk or harm available to the participants due to the nature of this study. However, as explained by authoritative literature, focusing on the topic, subject, or research methodology to assess or determine risk is insufficient.

The participant was given an explanation of what the study was about and that the only person to see the information was the researcher and doctoral committee comprising of three people. No personal information was questioned such as name, address, or phone number on the questionnaires or other written material used for the research data in order for the participants to remain autonomous. The researcher was the sole observer of individual material until all information was gathered into each of its categories to analyze and work results. Afterwards, the committee members were the only eligible individuals to see the unidentified data. Overall scores and other results are displayed in the dissertation and available for all to see.

Informed Consent

All participants were given an informed consent form (Appendix C) to read that (a) explained the study of why it was being conducted and (b) how the participant's privacy and confidentiality would be protected. The potential participant read the form and had the option to (a) continue with the questionnaire and EPPS test or (b) withdraw from the study.

Internet Research

Since time was a valuable resource for both types of entrepreneurs, the availability of completing the questionnaires was made by email. This particular practice enabled the participant to print the questionnaires, complete it, and mail them to a post office box to ensure data was not stolen. The participant had the contact information to notify the researcher if there were questions.

Questionnaire Design

There were two collection instruments that each participant completed. The first was a questionnaire developed by the researcher. It consisted of short answer and multiple-choice questions but worded for the specific entrepreneur participant (Appendix A and B). The second instrument was the Edwards Personal Preference Schedule (EPPS), which was given to all participants. This test consisted of 225 pairs of statements and the participant chose which statement she (a) may or may not like or (b) would be most likely or unlikely to do. There were no right or wrong answers.

Privacy and Confidentiality

After completion of the study, the data was stored in a locked cabinet that only has authorized access by the researcher. Research material stored for the minimum requirement of seven years will be burned so data cannot be traced. These procedures ensure privacy and confidentiality.

Validity and Reliability

The validity of this study appeared accurate for it clearly stated (a) the utilization of its own participants, (b) the requirements that the sample population adhered to, and (c) defined variables investigated in the Edwards Personal Preference Schedule (EPPS) that measured the psychological characteristics of the participants being investigated (Edwards, 1953). According to Edwards (1953), the reliability of this test was established by the creation of split-half coefficients or coefficients of internal consistency that determined the fifteen personality variables. Establishment was further verified when analyzing the data results. The statement variables were made in twos. If the EPPS test was filled consistently, the participant circled the same letter for both statement items. The consistency was verified by comparing the responses of both similar items. The highest consistency score that one could reach was 15. The highest, eligible score available for each psychological variable was 28.

CHAPTER 4. DATA COLLECTION AND ANALYSIS

The analysis of each research question aids in the understanding of the relationships between the two entrepreneur categories (a) World Athlete Entrepreneurs and (b) Women Business Entrepreneurs. The Ethnographic design of this case study gives the researcher the ability to investigate the relationship of variables and explore these variables seeking clues and patterns as described by Cooper and Schindler (2001). The quantitative nature of this study proves the relationship of variables and gives a better understanding of the data as discussed by Creswell (2002). He explains that the audience receives an improved analysis of the results by giving a complete picture.

This study targeted a total of sixty participants. This consisted of thirty World Athlete Entrepreneurs and thirty Women Business Entrepreneurs. Selective sampling was utilized in finding participants in both entrepreneur categories. This type of sampling format gave the ability to collect from known successful World Athlete Entrepreneurs and Woman Business Entrepreneurs. The sixty participants were found and given the studies; but fifty were returned. The participation of twenty-five participants in each category gave this study a 95% response rate for each group. The availability of having an even number of participation in each category still gives the study a reliable result.

The Edwards Personal Preference Schedule (EPPS) was given to World Athlete Entrepreneur and Women Business Entrepreneur participants with permission from David Edwards, the trustee of author, Allen L. Edwards living trust. This test investigates fifteen psychological and motivational variables; however, this study analyzed fourteen.

The development of two questionnaires by the researcher (Appendix A and B) consisted of the same questions but was worded to focus on the specific entrepreneur participant being interviewed. For example, question fifteen pertains to the birth theory. The World Athlete Entrepreneur questionnaire asks whether the participant comes from a rodeo or horse-oriented family. The Women Business Entrepreneur questionnaire asks whether the participant comes from a family who has an entrepreneurial background having owned or owns a business. This questionnaire collected data for additional motivational characteristics, business strategies, the Birth Theory, and Only or Eldest Daughter Syndrome. The validity and reliability aspects of the investigation was protected by asking the same questions to both participant categories.

Selected participants met requirement criteria to qualify for the study in order to get a reliable and valid result. The requirements are discussed in Chapter 3. The proper selection of participants allowed deliverance of the appropriate data to measure the objectives.

Data collection and analysis is organized and discussed by each research question.

Research question 1

Are Women Business Entrepreneurs and World Athlete Entrepreneurs successful?

Analysis of the variables accumulated from research question 2 and 3 find many similar characteristics shared by World Athlete Entrepreneurs and Women Business Entrepreneurs in measuring success. These will be introduced starting with the next research question.

Garret (2006) stated a successful entrepreneur's work is their passion and this was expressed by both participant categories in this study. The other three factors stated by both World Athlete Entrepreneurs and Women Business Entrepreneurs relate to the entrepreneur definition described in the *definition of terms* in chapter 1 (a) train or consult others (self-actualization and achievement), (b) reputation (self-actualization), and (c) monetary value (achievement and capital). Additional findings show Women Business Entrepreneurs receive success for the ability to keep business coming through the door. Their business is from customers, advertising, and other promotional techniques. This is to promote financial freedom and retirement goals. World Athlete Entrepreneurs seek for financial freedom by getting to a success level of training barrel horses and other riders, holding clinics, development of training instruction aids, and receiving financial gain from sponsorships and endorsements.

Research question 2

How do Women Business Entrepreneurs and World Athlete Entrepreneurs measure success?

The World Athlete Entrepreneur and Women Business Entrepreneur questionnaires ask this as an open-ended question of how each participant measures her success. Each participant listed her personal traits or factors. The findings were interesting in observing the similarity of answers between the two entrepreneur categories. World Athlete Entrepreneurs and Women Business Entrepreneurs listed these same success measuring factors (a) internal motivation, (b) drive, (c) continuing education, (d) compassion, (e) hard work, (f) taking things seriously, (g) commitment, (h) talent and creativity, (i) determination, (j) energy, (k) endurance, (l) supportive family and spouse, (m) competitiveness, (n) persistence, (o) job continuation, (p) quality, (q) positive thinking and attitude, (r) confidence, (s) communication, (t) financial rewards,

38

(u) trainers/mentors, (v) time and flexibility, (w) reputation, (x) teaching and being able to help others, (y) God, and (z) goal setting and achievement. Additional factors were listed separately under each entrepreneur category. The World Athlete Entrepreneur stated (a) dedication, (b) health of horse and self, (c) independence, (d) experience, and (e) organization. The Women Business Entrepreneur listed (a) perfection, (b) ability not to work for others, (c) integrity, and (d) accuracy. An association of the success-measuring factors discussed relates to past research studies discussed in the chapter 2 literature review.

Important factors discussed by established and well-known World Athlete Entrepreneurs included (a) continuing education, (b) surrounding one self with people who believe in you, (c) studying the craft, (d) finding an area to become successful, (e) being creative, and (f) being consistent in philosophy.

Research Question 3

What are the psychological and motivational traits shared by a World Athlete Entrepreneur and a Woman Business Entrepreneur?

Motivational characteristics. The literature review discussed various reasons of why a person enters the entrepreneur venture. Eight common characteristics listed in the literature review were included on both the World Athlete Entrepreneur and the Women Business Entrepreneur questionnaires. Participants had the choice of circling one or more reasons of her motivation to start.

The collected findings are different from past research literature claiming the main reason Women Business Entrepreneurs and professional athletes start their own endeavor is to (a) utilize a skill or talent, (b) fulfill a passion, or (c) for the high need of

39

achievement. According to the findings of this study, figure 1 suggests Women Business Entrepreneurs start up businesses for (a) flexibility, (b) utilize a skill or talent, and (c) fulfill a passion. The top three motivational choices of World Athlete Entrepreneurs are (a) to fulfill a passion, (b) to utilize a skill or talent, and (c) a high need for achievement. Findings suggest the two entrepreneur groups are different with the need for high achievement. Findings showing flexibility to be a main motivational target for Women Business Entrepreneurs relate to past studies claiming flexibility to be an additional, attractive factor. The other characteristics or variables, as shown in figure 1, display a small difference between the two entrepreneurs; however, both entrepreneurs are low in considering start up for gaining confidence.

Chi-Square tests (displayed in Appendix E - L) were conducted to confirm an association of these motivational variables between the two independent variables a) World Athlete Entrepreneurs and b) Women Business Entrepreneurs. The analyses displays .2 significance level (rounded off) for each motivational characteristic except for the *to gain confidence* variable. This result rejects the null hypothesis based on the acceptable range of deviation $p > .1$

Null Hypothesis: There is no association of motivational characteristics between World Athlete Entrepreneurs and Women Business Entrepreneurs.

Alternative Hypothesis: There is an association of motivational characteristics between World Athlete Entrepreneurs and Women Business Entrepreneurs.

Psychological characteristics. The Edwards Personal Preference Schedule collected additional motivational characteristics of both entrepreneurs. Each individual

EPPS test was scored for each variable investigated and transferred to the SPSS program for further analysis.

Cross Tabulations (displayed in Appendix Q - DD) and Chi-Square tests (displayed in this section) were used to measure the association of each individual variable between the independent variables (a) World Athlete Entrepreneurs (represented by the number one) and (b) Women Business Entrepreneurs (represented by the number 2). The cross tabulation tables display the percentage of each entrepreneur type that scored a particular value for each characteristic. These values are displayed in the first column. The maximum score eligible to be received for each dependent variable was a 28. Pearson chi-square tests were used to analyze the data for each individual psychological variable in order to reject or accept the null hypothesis.

Null hypothesis: There is not an association in each particular psychological variable between the two independent variables (a) World Athlete Entrepreneurs and (b) Women Business Entrepreneurs.

Alternative hypothesis: There is an association in each particular psychological variable between the two independent variables (a) World Athlete Entrepreneurs and (b) Women Business Entrepreneurs.

The null hypothesis is accepted based on $p > .05$; however, $p > .1$ is an acceptable range of deviation.

Appendix EE displays the Mean for each psychological variable scored by World Athlete Entrepreneurs (represented by 1) and Women Business Entrepreneurs (represented by 2). It gives a visual presentation of scrutinizing each dependent variable means between the two groups investigated.

41

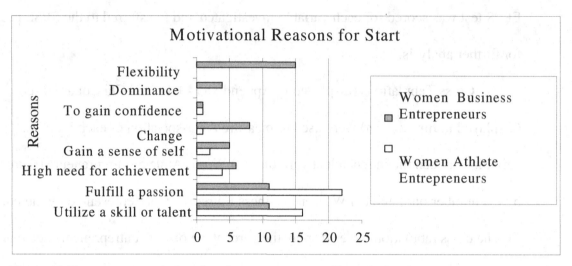

Figure 1. Entrepreneur motivational start up comparison chart.

Abasement variable.

Null Hypothesis: There is no association of the abasement characteristic between the two independent variables (a) World Athlete Entrepreneurs and (b) Women Business Entrepreneurs.

Alternative Hypothesis: There is an association of the abasement characteristic between the two independent variables (a) World Athlete Entrepreneurs and (b) Women Business Entrepreneurs.

The chi-square analysis displayed in table 1 calculated a significance level of .1 (rounded off). This suggests that the null hypothesis is rejected based on the acceptable range of deviation, $p > .1$.

Achievement variable.

Null Hypothesis: There is no association of the achievement characteristic between the two independent variables (a) World Athlete Entrepreneurs and (b) Women Business Entrepreneurs.

42

Alternative Hypothesis: There is an association of the achievement characteristic between the two independent variables (a) World Athlete Entrepreneurs and (b) Women Business Entrepreneurs.

The chi-square analysis displayed in table 2 calculated a significance level of .4 (rounded off). This suggests the null hypothesis is rejected based on the acceptable range of deviation, $p > .1$.

Affiliation variable

Null Hypothesis: There is no association of the affiliation characteristic between the two independent variables (a) World Athlete Entrepreneurs and (b) Women Business Entrepreneurs.

Alternative Hypothesis: There is an association of the affiliation characteristic between the two independent variables (a) World Athlete Entrepreneurs and (b) Women Business Entrepreneurs.

The chi-square analysis displayed in table 3 calculated the significance level of .4 (rounded off). This finding suggests that the null hypothesis is rejected based on the acceptable range of deviation, $p > .1$.

Aggression variable.

Null hypothesis: There is no association of the aggression characteristic between the two independent variables (a) World Athlete Entrepreneurs and (b) Women Business Entrepreneurs.

Alternative hypothesis: There is an association of the aggression characteristic between the two independent variables (a) World Athlete Entrepreneurs and (b) Women Business Entrepreneurs.

43

The chi-square analysis displayed in table 4 calculated a significance level of .7 (rounded off). This suggests that the null hypothesis is rejected based on the acceptable range of deviation $p > .1$.

Autonomy variable.

Null Hypothesis: There is no association of the autonomy characteristic between the two independent variables (a) World Athlete Entrepreneurs and (b) Women Business Entrepreneurs.

Alternative Hypothesis: There is an association of the autonomy characteristic between the two independent variables (a) World Athlete Entrepreneurs and (b) Women Business Entrepreneurs.

The chi-square analysis displayed in table 5 calculated a significance level of .4 (rounded off). This suggests that the null hypothesis is rejected based on the acceptable range of deviation $p > .1$.

Change variable.

Null Hypothesis: There is no association of the change variable between the two independent variables (a) World Athlete Entrepreneur and (b) Women Business Entrepreneur.

Alternative Hypothesis: There is an association of the change variable between the two independent variables (a) World Athlete Entrepreneurs and (b) Women Business Entrepreneurs.

The chi-square analysis displayed in table 6 calculated a significance level of .4 (rounded off). This suggests the null hypothesis is rejected based on the acceptance range of deviation $p > .1$.

Table 1.

Abasement Chi-Square Test

	Value	df	Asymp. Sig. (2-sided)
Pearson chi-square	24.219 [a]	17	.114
Likelihood Ratio	32.431	17	.013
N of Valid Cases	50		

Note. 36 cells (100.0%) have expected count less than 5. The minimum expected count is .50.

Table 2.

Achievement Chi-Square test

	Value	df	Asymp. Sig. (2-sided)
Pearson chi-square	19.200 [a]	18	.380
Likelihood Ratio	25.128	18	.121
N of Valid Cases	50		

Note. 38 cells (100.0%) have expected count less than 5. The minimum expected count is .50.

Table 3.

Affiliation Chi-Square Test

	Value	df	Asymp. Sig. (2-sided)
Pearson chi-square	19.133 [a]	18	.384
Likelihood Ratio	24.207	18	.148
N of Valid Cases	50		

Note. 38 cells (100.0%) have expected count less than 5. The minimum expected count is .50.

Table 4.

Aggression Chi-Square Test

	Value	df	Asymp. Sig. (2-sided)
Pearson chi-square	16.000 [a]	19	.657
Likelihood Ratio	20.526	19	.364
N of Valid Cases	50		

Note. 40 cells (100.0%) have expected count less than 5. The minimum expected count is .50.

Table 5.

Autonomy Chi-Square Test

	Value	df	Asymp. Sig. (2-sided)
Pearson chi-square	18.200 [a]	17	.376
Likelihood Ratio	24.081	17	.117
N of Valid Cases	50		

Note. 36 cells (100.0%) have expected count less than 5. The minimum expected count is .50.

Deference variable.

Null Hypothesis: There is no association of the deference characteristic between the two independent variables (a) World Athlete Entrepreneurs and (b) Women Business Entrepreneurs.

Alternative Hypothesis: There is an association of the deference characteristic between the two independent variables (a) World Athlete Entrepreneurs and (b) Women Business Entrepreneurs.

46

The chi-square analysis displayed in table 7 calculated a significance level of .09 This suggests that the null hypothesis is accepted based on the acceptable range of deviation, $p > .1$

Dominance Variable.

Null Hypothesis: There is no association of the dominance characteristic between the two independent variables (a) World Athlete Entrepreneurs and (b) Women Business Entrepreneurs.

Alternative Hypothesis: There is an association of the dominance characteristic between the two independent variables (a) World Athlete Entrepreneurs and (b) Women Business Entrepreneurs.

The chi-square Analysis displayed in table 8 calculated a significance level of .5 (rounded off). This suggests that the null hypothesis is rejected based on the acceptable range of deviation, $p > .1$.

Endurance variable.

Null Hypothesis: There is no association of the Endurance characteristic between the two independent variables (a) World Athlete Entrepreneurs and (b) Women Business Entrepreneurs.

Alternative Hypothesis: There is an association of the Endurance characteristic between the two independent variables (a) World Athlete Entrepreneurs and (b) Women Business Entrepreneurs.

The chi-square analysis displayed in table 9 calculated a significance level of .8 (rounded off). This suggests that the null hypothesis is rejected on the basis of the acceptable range of deviation, $p > .1$.

Exhibition variable.

Null hypothesis: There is no association of the exhibition characteristic between the two independent variables (a) World Athlete Entrepreneurs and (b) Women Business Entrepreneurs.

Alternative hypothesis: There is an association of the exhibition characteristic between the two independent variable (a) World Athlete Entrepreneurs and (b) Women Business Entrepreneurs.

The chi-square analysis displayed in table 10 calculated a significance level of .4 (rounded off). This suggests that the null hypothesis is rejected based on the accepted range of deviation, $p > .1$.

Intraception variable.

Null Hypothesis: There is no association of the intraception characteristic between the two independent variables (a) World Athlete Entrepreneurs and (b) Women Business Entrepreneurs.

Alternative Hypothesis: There is an association of the intraception characteristic between the two independent variables (a) World Athlete Entrepreneurs and (b) Women Business Entrepreneurs.

The chi-square analysis displayed in table 11 calculated a significance level of .5 (rounded off). This suggests the null hypothesis is rejected based on the acceptable range of deviation, $p > .1$.

Nurturance variable.

Null Hypothesis: There is no association of the nurturance characteristic between the two independent variables (a) World Athlete Entrepreneurs and (b) Women Business Entrepreneurs.

Alternative Hypothesis: There is an association of the nurturance characteristic between the two independent variables (a) World Athlete Entrepreneurs and (b) Women Business Entrepreneurs.

The chi-square analysis displayed in table 12 calculated a significance level of .9 (rounded off). This suggests the null hypothesis is rejected based on the accepted range of deviation, $p > .1$.

Order variable.

Null Hypothesis: There is no association of the order characteristic between the two independent variables (a) World Athlete Entrepreneurs and (b) Women Business Entrepreneurs.

Alternative Hypothesis: There is an association of the order characteristic between the two independent variables (a) World Athlete Entrepreneurs and (b) Women Business Entrepreneurs.

The chi-square analysis displayed in table 13 calculated a significance level of .5 (rounded off). This suggests the null hypothesis is rejected based on the accepted range of deviation, $p > .1$

Succorance variable.

Null Hypothesis: There is no association of the succorance characteristic between the two independent variables (a) World Athlete Entrepreneurs and (b) Women Business Entrepreneurs.

Alternative Hypothesis: There is an association of the succorance characteristic between the two independent variables (a) World Athlete Entrepreneurs and (b) Women Business Entrepreneurs.

The chi-square analysis displayed in table 14 calculated a significance level of .3 (rounded off). This suggests the null hypothesis is rejected based on the accepted range of deviation, $p > .1$.

Table 6.

Change Chi-Square Test

	Value	df	Asymp. Sig. (2-sided)
Pearson chi-square	19.133 [a]	18	.384
Likelihood Ratio	25.759	18	.105
N of Valid Cases	50		

Note. 38 cells (100.0%) have expected count less than 5. The minimum expected count is .50.

Table 7.

Deference Chi-Square Test

	Value	df	Asymp. Sig. (2-sided)
Pearson chi-square	24.000 [a]	16	.090
Likelihood Ratio	31.075	16	.013
N of Valid Cases	50		

Note. 34 cells (100.0%) have expected count less than 5. The minimum expected count is .50.

Table 8.

Dominance Chi-Square Test

	Value	df	Asymp. Sig. (2-sided)
Pearson chi-square	15.733 [a]	17	.543
Likelihood Ratio	20.490	17	.250
N of Valid Cases	50		

Note. 36 cells (100.0%) have expected count less than 5. The minimum expected count is .50.

Table 9.

Endurance Chi-Square Test

	Value	df	Asymp Sig. (2-side)
Pearson chi-square	13.533 [a]	18	.759
Likelihood Ratio	17.489	18	.490
N of Valid Cases	50		

Note. 38 cells (100.0%) have expected count less than 5. The minimum expected count is .50.

Table 10.

Exhibition Chi-Square Test

	Value	df	Asymp. Sig. (2-sided)
Pearson chi-square	13.886 [a]	13	.382
Likelihood	17.888	13	.162
N of Valid Cases	50		

Note. 28 cells (100.0%) have expected count less than 5. The minimum expected count is .50.

Table 11.

Intraception Chi-Square Test

	Value	df	Asymp. Sig. (2-sided)
Pearson chi-square	12.673 [a]	13	.473
Likelihood Ratio	14.659	13	.329
N of Valid Cases	50		

Note. 28 cells (100.0%) have expected count less than 5. The minimum expected count is .50.

Table 12.

Nurturance Chi-Square Test

	Value	df	Asymp. Sig. (2-sided)
Pearson chi-square	10.333 [a]	17	.889
Likelihood Ratio	12.852	17	.746
N of Valid Cases	50		

Note. 36 cells (100.0%) have expected count less than 5. The minimum expected count is .50.

Table 13.

Order Chi-Square Test

	Value	df	Asymp Sig. (2-sidd)
Pearson chi-square	14.867 [a]	15	.461
Likelihod Ratio	18.939	15	.217
N of Valid Cases	50		

Note. 32 cells (100.0%) have expected count less than 5. The minimum expected count is .50.

Table 14.

Succorance Chi-Square Test

	Value	df	Asymp Sig. (2sided)
Pearson chi-square	19.867 [a]	18	.340
Likelihood Ratio	26.541	18	.088
N of Valid Cases	50		

Note. 38 cells (100.0%) have expected count less than 5. The minimum expected count is .50.

Research Question 4

What human and social capital factors do World Athlete Entrepreneurs and Women Business Entrepreneurs attain (e.g. age, experience, and education)?

Human capital. The analysis of data gathered from World Athlete Entrepreneur and Women Business Entrepreneur questionnaires displays an age difference between the two entrepreneur categories. Table 15 displays the data that suggests Women Business Entrepreneurs are more successful between the ages of 45 – 50. World Athlete Entrepreneurs are of a different status having a tie between the 18 – 25, 39 – 44, and 51-56 categories.

53

Experience. Findings gathered from both entrepreneur questionnaires suggest experience to be another factor in considering success for the World Athlete Entrepreneur and the Woman Business Entrepreneur. The data suggests Women Business Entrepreneurs do not take as long reaching success level. Table 16 proposes Women Business Entrepreneurs arrive at success level in a minimum of five years. The World Athlete Entrepreneur differs in this relation due to the data recommending success is dependent on the years of experience. Findings show World Athlete Entrepreneurs to arrive at success level at a minimum of eleven years.

Education. The data gathered from World Athlete Entrepreneur and Women Business Entrepreneur questionnaires were analyzed and sorted in table 17. The table presents an overall summary of the educational level of each type of entrepreneur. The table distinguishes the type of entrepreneur by the representation of *WAE* for World Athlete Entrepreneurs and *WBE* for Women Business Entrepreneurs. The education level is stated in the first column of the table; which, is represented by rows (a) row 1 stands for no high school completion, (b) row 2 stands for high school completion, (c) row 3 stands for GED completion, (d) row 4 stands for associate of arts degree or associate of science completion, (e) row 5 stands for bachelor's degree completion, (f) row 6 stands for master's degree completion, (g) row 7 stands for PhD (doctorate of philosophy) degree completion, and (h) row 8 represents pursuing or completion of a professional license.

The data of education level presented in table 17 and figure 2 displays a visual presentation of the data decision suggesting a significant difference in the education level of the two entrepreneur categories. World Athlete Entrepreneurs are found to hold high school diplomas where Women Business Entrepreneurs are found to hold higher education with the associate of arts/associate of science or bachelor's degree being the norm. However, a distinguishing factor is the high amount of participants in the World Athlete Entrepreneur category that hold bachelor's degrees. This corresponds to literature finding many athletes seeking and obtaining bachelor's degrees in their pursuit of success.

Social capital. Both types of entrepreneurs explicitly articulated on the World Athlete Entrepreneur questionnaire and the Women Business Entrepreneur questionnaire that social capital is an important factor in success. Participants continuously enounced (a) networking, (b) being known, (c) having a valuable reputation, and (d) being able to help others are very important. World Athlete Entrepreneurs explained various practices of this social capital. Findings show that networking for World Athlete Entrepreneurs is Table 15.

Age Comparison of Both Entrepreneur Types in Reaching Success

AGE	World Athlete Entrepreneur	Women Business Entrepreneur
18 - 25	5	0
26-31	3	0
32-38	4	2
39-44	5	6
45-50	3	10
51-56	5	2
57+		5

Table 16.

Years of Experience of Both Entrepreneur Types in Reaching Success

Experience	Years	World Athlete Entrepreneur	Woman Business Entrepreneur
	Under 5 yrs	0	7
	5-10 yrs	0	8
	11-15 yrs	5	3
	16-20 yrs	7	4
	21-25 yrs	3	2
	26-30 yrs	10	1

Table 17.

Educational Level Case Summary Comparison

	PERSON					
	WAE		WBE		Total	
		Total		Total		
	1	n	2	n	N	
NOHS	.		1	1	1	
HS	10	1	3	1	2	
GED	0	1	0	1	2	
AAORAS	3	1	6	1	2	
BA	8	1	6	1	2	
MA	0	1	4	1	2	
PHD	0	1	1	1	2	
PROFLI	4	1	4	1	2	

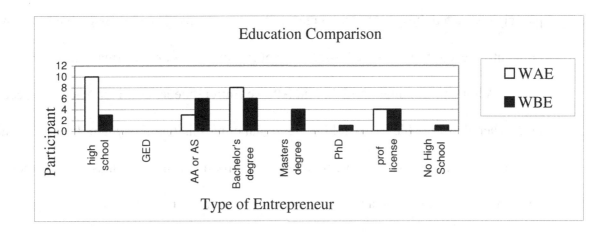

Figure 2: Educational Level Case Summary Comparison

used to be further educated with important aspects in the (a) barrel racing industry with

mentor/trainers and (b) other horse type industries to keep up with equipment, training

methods, equine health issues, quality horses, and other relevant aspects of the sporting

business. Women Business Entrepreneurs expressed networking to be of importance and

illustrated similar practices by staying educated with various business issues by

participating on association boards and having mentors. In summary, both entrepreneurs

claim continuing education as an overall importance in both industries.

Research Question 5

What kinds of financial availability do World Athlete Entrepreneurs and Women

Business Entrepreneurs use during their venture?

The analysis of data gathered from the World Athlete Entrepreneur questionnaire

and the Women Business Entrepreneur questionnaire recommends both entrepreneur

types are similar in their financial business strategy. The data assembled indicates both

types of entrepreneurs rely on bootstrapping techniques and utilize business angels to keep their venture financed. Three out of the twenty-five Women Business Entrepreneur participants stated they were able to receive business loans. The data assembled indicates both entrepreneur types utilize business angels as another source of financing.

Additional findings show World Athlete Entrepreneurs consider reaching success level when they are able to (a) hold professional clinics and gain payment for additional instructional methods; (b) receive royalties from product designs such as tack, clothes, and other equine products; and (c) receive money from sponsorships and endorsements.

Research question 6

Are both women entrepreneurs employed in other disciplines for additional financing?

The data retrieved from World Athlete Entrepreneur and Women Business Entrepreneur questionnaires indicate World Athlete Entrepreneurs to have a higher probability to hold additional jobs to help in the finance of their venture as displayed in figure 3.

Additional data analysis exemplifies most second jobs held by World Athlete Entrepreneurs are in professional or self-employed careers as illustrated in figure 4. Horse related careers follow closely in range. The professional variable includes career positions such as (a) engineers, (b) executive and administrative assistants, (c) management, (d) state officers, and (e) medical professions. The horse-related career consists of various equine career positions such as working in feed stores, veterinary hospitals, and other equine services. The self-employed variable consists of horse-related careers or professional services stated above.

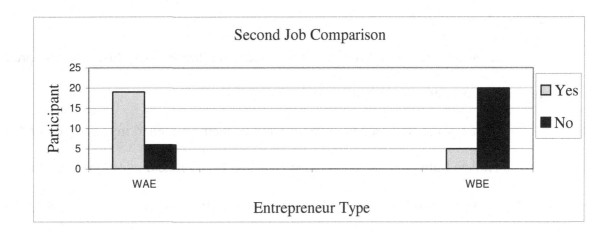

Figure 3: Second job comparisons of World Athlete Entrepreneurs and Women Business Entrepreneurs. World Athlete Entrepreneurs are more likely to hold second jobs.

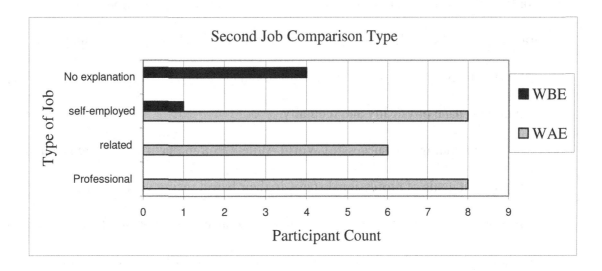

Figure 4: Second job comparison type. The type of second job that each entrepreneur type has.

Research Question 7

How does the World Athlete Entrepreneur and the Women Business Entrepreneur practice the strategic art of benchmarking?

Participants discussed the various ways of their benchmarking strategies on the World Athlete Entrepreneur and Women Business Entrepreneur questionnaires. In summary, networking with the competition and realistic goal setting seem to play a big part for both entrepreneur groups. Personal improvement is watched in both areas to learn from mistakes and observe the bottom line. Additional benchmarking strategies by the World Athlete Entrepreneur is (a) extensive studies of trade publications, (b) measuring competition runs against the toughest barrel racer at each competition to help select training ethics that will yield a higher rate of success, (c) having a great support system, (d) watching personal videos of competition runs to analyze for improvement, and (e) keeping in shape physically and mentally.

The findings for successful World Athlete Entrepreneurs having reached their achievement goals of professional status in their barrel racing venture utilize benchmarking by (a) analyzing their clinic attendance; (b) analyzing the possibility of producing new clinic programs; (c) evaluating and comparing the sales of equine products such as vitamins and supplements, tack, and clothes endorsed; (d) the selling of instructional aids; and (e) the calling for written articles.

Women Business Entrepreneurs keep a close eye on every aspect of business. They (a) set goals and are prepared to make alternative changes when needed; (b) keep overhead low so business is profitable; (c) compare local and national businesses; (d) set monthly, semi-monthly, and yearly goals; (e) form business plans; (f) participate on

association boards; (g) track customer sales; and (h) evaluate client satisfaction.

Research Question 8

Do Women Business Entrepreneurs and World Athlete Entrepreneurs experience

the same barriers (a) financial issues, (b) family, and (c) genetic stereotyping?

The World Athlete Entrepreneur and Women Business Entrepreneur

questionnaires asked questions pertaining to each variable being investigated.

Financial. The World Athlete Entrepreneur and Women Business Entrepreneur

questionnaires asked the participants in an open-ended question if there are any barriers

that appear while pursuing their venture. Eight World Athlete Entrepreneurs and two

Women Business Entrepreneurs claimed to have financial barriers. It was discussed in

research question 5 that bootstrapping techniques seem to play a major role with both

entrepreneur groups.

Family. The data displayed in figure 5 suggests both entrepreneur types to be

married. According to data responses, both entrepreneur types receive family support but

no support was given at the beginning of their venture due to being in a single status at

that particular time.

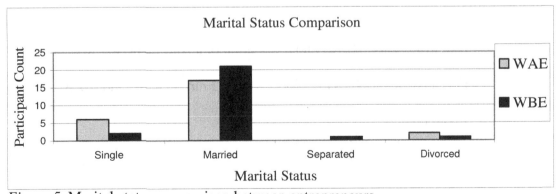

Figure 5. Marital status comparison between entrepreneurs

61

A chi-square test was performed to accept or reject the null hypothesis that there are no associations with family support between the independent variables (a) World Athlete Entrepreneurs and (b) Women Business Entrepreneurs. The chi-square analysis (displayed in Appendix M - P) calculated a significance level of .2 (rounded off) for each dependent variable (a) single, (b) married, (c) separated, and (d) divorced. This finding rejects the null hypothesis based on the acceptable range of deviation, $p > .1$.

Children: The World Athlete Entrepreneur and Women Business Entrepreneur questionnaire gathered the data to compare the number of children each participant has. These statistics were analyzed in a chi-square test where findings accepted the null hypothesis of not having an association as shown in table 18. The cross tabulation data found in table 19 suggests World Athlete Entrepreneurs are most likely not to have children. If so, she will have one. The majority of Women Business Entrepreneurs have at least two children.

Children are claimed to be another type of family barrier for both entrepreneurs by past research studies and authoritative literature. These studies suggest women entrepreneurs having to wait till the children are older to pursue an endeavor. This research study analyzed this philosophy and conducted a chi-square test to confirm an association.

Null hypothesis: There is no association of a waiting period with the two independent variables (a) World Athlete Entrepreneurs and (b) Women Business Entrepreneurs.

Alternative hypothesis: There is an association of a waiting period with the two independent variables (a) World Athlete Entrepreneurs and (b) Women Business Entrepreneurs.

A comparison count of which entrepreneur type did or did not wait is displayed in table 20. The chi-square test in table 21 calculated a significance level of .3 (rounded off). The results displayed in table 21 rejected the null hypothesis based on the acceptable range of deviation, $p > .1$.

Genetic Stereotyping. Women Business Entrepreneurs stated that they have experienced genetic stereotyping through their entrepreneur endeavor. Their experience has included (a) not being eligible to attend men's functions where a lot of business is and done by the *good ole' boys network*, (b) assumption of higher expectations, (c) experiencing negative perceptions about strong women, (d) experiencing negativity from other women, (e) experienced resentment from male managers, (f) experience resentment from male employees, and (g) experience with male customers or salesmen automatically assuming that *a man* owns the business.

World Athlete Entrepreneurs stated that men have more opportunities at the very top and are more recognized. Additional barriers included on the questionnaires for World Athlete Entrepreneurs are (a) time management, (b) self-criticism or discipline, (c) health and safety of both horse and rider, (d) keeping priorities straight, (e) balancing family and college with barrel racing, and (f) keeping up with competition growth. Women Business Entrepreneurs experience similar barriers in (a) time management, (b) health and disability issues, (c) finding good employees, (d) keeping continuous business,

63

(e) changing technology, (f) distractions, (g) inability to say no to unrelated tasks, (h)

avoiding necessary tasks such as marketing, and (i) letting customers dictate charges.

Table 18.

Number of Children Chi Square Data Analysis

	Value	df	Asymp. Sig. (2-sided)
Pearson chi-square	27.050 [a]	5	.000
Likelihood Ratio	32.648	5	.000
N of Valid Cases	50		

Note. 6 cells (50.0%) have expected count less than 5. The minimum expected count is
.50.

Table 19.

Number of Children Cross Tabulation Table

		WAE	WBE	Total
NOFCHILD	0	10		10
	1	10	2	12
	2	3	13	16
	3	1	5	6
	4	1	4	5
	5		1	1
Total		25	25	50

Table 20.

Waiting Period Cross Tabulation

		yes	no	not applicable	Total
PERSON	WAE	5	10	10	25
	WBE	6	14	5	25
Total		11	24	15	50

Table 21.

Waiting Period Chi-Square Test

	Value	df	Asymp. Sig. (2-sided)
Pearson chi-square	2.424 [a]	2	.298
Likelihood Ratio	2.460	2	.292
N of Valid Cases	50		

Note. 0 cells (.0%) have expected count less than 5. The minimum expected count is 5.50.

Research question 9

Do World Athlete Entrepreneurs and Women Business Entrepreneurs share the same birth theory or eldest/daughter syndrome?

Oldest or Eldest Daughter Syndrome. The chi-square test analyzed data retrieved from the World Athlete Entrepreneur and Women Business Entrepreneur questionnaires. The results shown in Tables 22 and 24 displays World Athlete Entrepreneurs and Women Business Entrepreneurs are higher in number for *not* being an only or eldest daughter.

The chi-square tests displayed in tables 23 and 25 calculated a significance level of .7 (rounded off) for the only daughter variable and a .8 (rounded off) for the eldest daughter variable. These findings suggest that the null hypothesis is rejected based on the accepted range of deviation, $p > .1$.

Null hypothesis: There is no association of the Only/Eldest Daughter Syndrome with the two independent variables (a) World Athlete Entrepreneurs and (b) Women Business Entrepreneurs.

Alternative hypothesis: There is an association of the Only/Eldest Daughter Syndrome with the two independent variables (a) World Athlete Entrepreneurs and (b) Women Business Entrepreneurs.

Birth theory. Past research studies claim that entrepreneurs are from families with similar entrepreneurial backgrounds. On either questionnaire, participants were asked whether she was from a family with a rodeo or other horse industry background (e.g. World Athlete Entrepreneur) or a family that owns or has owned their own business (e.g. Women Business Entrepreneur). The data implies a decision that it is customary to find both types of entrepreneurs coming from families of correlative backgrounds. The chi-square test analyzed the gathered data from the questionnaires in order to find whether there is an association of the birth theory between the two independent variables (a) World Athlete Entrepreneurs and (b) Women Business Entrepreneurs.

Null hypothesis: There is no association of the birth theory between the two independent variables (a) World Athlete Entrepreneurs and (b) Women Business Entrepreneurs.

66

Alternative hypothesis: There is an association of the birth theory between the two independent variables (a) World Athlete Entrepreneurs and (b) Women Business Entrepreneurs.

The chi-square test displayed in Table 26 calculated a significance level of 1. The null hypothesis is rejected based on an accepted range of deviation, $p > .1$.

Table 22.

Only Daughter Cross Tabulation

		WAE	WBE	Total
ONLY	yes	4	3	7
	no	21	22	43
Total		25	25	50

Table 23.

Only Daughter Chi-Square Test

	Value	df	Asymp. Sig. (2-sided)	Exact Sig. (2-sided)	Exact Sig. (1-sided)
Pearson chi-square [a]	.16	1	.68		
Continuity	.00	1	1.00		
Likelihood	.16	1	.68		
Fisher's Exact				1.00	.50
N of Valid	50				

Note. Computed only for a 2x2 table

Note. 2 cells (50.0%) have expected count less than 5. The minimum expected count is 3.50.

Table 24.

Eldest Daughter Cross Tabulation

		WAE	WBE	Total
ELDEST	yes	8	9	17
	no	17	16	33
Total		25	25	50

Table 25.

Eldest Daughter Chi-Square Tests

	Value	df	Asymp. (2-	Exact Sig. (2-sided)	Exact Sig. (1-sided)
Pearson chi-square	.089[b]	1	.765		
Continuity [a]	.000	1	1.000		
Likelihood	.089	1	.765		
Fisher's Exact				1.000	.500
N of Valid	50				

Note. Computed only for a 2x2 table

Note. 0 cells (.0%) have expected count less than 5. The minimum expected count is 8.50.

Table 26.

Birth Theory Chi-Square

	Value	df	Asymp. Sig. (2-sided)	Exact (2-sided)	Exact (1-sided)
Pearson chi-square	.000[b]	1	1.00		
Continuity	.000	1	1.00		
Likelihood	.000	1	1.00		
Fisher's Exact				1.00	.616
N of Valid	50				

Note. Computed only for a 2x2

Note. 0 cells (.0%) have expected count less than 5. The minimum expected count is 9.00.

CHAPTER 5. RESULTS, CONCLUSIONS, AND RECOMMENDATIONS

The purpose of this study was to compare and contrast Women Barrel Racers with Women Business Entrepreneurs and determine if there is an association between women who race and women who have their own businesses.

The qualitative part of this study has demanded a strong commitment of time and resources from the researcher; however, as Creswell explains, the ethnographic experience of the study allowed for a collection of details and other important data to help interpret and confirm similarities of behavior and belief patterns of World Athlete Entrepreneurs and Women Business Entrepreneurs (2002). The quantitative experience has justified established associations between these two groups.

This present perspective study is of an ideological nature allowing for a feminist approach. It gives the researcher a position of what Creswell refers to as a *critical ethnographer.* This allows the researcher to speak for World Athlete Entrepreneurs in order to promote action and bring a change to the general society and business professionals (1998, 2002). It is found that society remains unaware of past research studies regarding entrepreneurial levels of athletes. However, these past studies target males such as Pearson and Haney's (1999) study concluding cowboys to be entrepreneurs.

The passing of women rights has helped women with many opportunities; however, society continues to characterize and stereotype. Therefore, women are expected to behave according to the way it rules. In addition, women tend to experience higher expectations in regards to business and athleticism.

This chapter discusses the findings and conclusions organized by research questions. It continues with a summary of the chapter discussion. To conclude recommendations are made to (a) society and business professionals, (b) World Athlete Entrepreneurs, and (c) researchers.

Research Question 1 and 2

Are Women Business Entrepreneurs and World Athlete Entrepreneurs successful? How do Women Business Entrepreneurs and World Athlete Entrepreneurs measure success?

Sage (1993) concludes there is no definite formula to measure success. Researchers interpret their suggestion of what true success is. Danco (1993) suggests true success is being able to continue the business or activity. The particular, individual entrepreneur has his or her personal goals and a definition of achievement that determine success. The *definition of terms* in chapter one explains an entrepreneur to be a person participating in his or her own activity to obtain capital, self-actualization, and achievement. He or she is responsible for his or her own financial resources to pay for expenses in order to continue their venture. In essence, according to this explanation, it is assumed that the measuring factors in determining entrepreneurial success are (a) financial being, (b) self-actualization, and (c) achievement.

The World Athlete Entrepreneur and the Women Business Entrepreneur questionnaires asked in the form of an open-ended question about the factors or characteristics that determine each participant's success. The three frequently success factors stated by both World Athlete Entrepreneurs and Women Business Entrepreneurs relate to the entrepreneur definition (a) train or consult others (self-actualization and achievement), (b) reputation (self-actualization and achievement), and (c) monetary value (achievement and financial being). These factors are distinguished by the specific industry jargon but each has the same logistics. The monetary value can be derived from various events depending on the specific industry. For example, World Athlete Entrepreneurs gain financial resources from (a) winnings, training horses, giving lessons, and/or clinics; (b) receiving money or other benefits from sponsorships and endorsements; and (c) royalties from the sales of their product designs (tack, clothing, and horse supplements). Women Business Entrepreneurs are similar to all three of these as they gain their monetary value from sales and making profits. These can be achieved by (a) purchases of products they carry, (b) purchases of their own product designs or services, and (c) sales of customers brought in from advertising. Both entrepreneurs have the necessity of (a) keeping the customer coming through the door, (b) meeting the supply and demand, and (c) the ability to keep up with the competition in the marketplace in order to reach a success level.

It is recommended that both entrepreneur types are similar with their interpretation of accomplishment. The research determined both entrepreneurs are successful in their ability to continue their endeavor. The World Athlete Entrepreneur seeks alternate business strategies to continue competition if appropriate. If she is a trainer and/or instructor, she has to promote her training skills better than the other trainers and prove herself as an instructor to keep clients coming through her door. As one participant claimed on her questionnaire, she feels she has to be at the very top of her particular field because men have more opportunities and are more recognized. The *keeping up with competition* is a continuing factor for both World Athlete Entrepreneurs and Women Business Entrepreneurs.

World Athlete Entrepreneurs and Women Business Entrepreneurs participating in this study included correlative success measuring factors such as (a) internal motivation, (b) drive, (c) continuing education, (d) compassion, (e) hard work, (f) taking things seriously, (g) commitment, (h) talent and creativity, (i) determination, (j) energy, (k) endurance, (l) supportive family and spouse, (m) competitiveness, (n) persistence, (o) job continuation, (p) quality, (q) positive thinking and attitude, (r) confidence, (s) communication, (t) financial rewards, (u) trainers/mentors, (v) time and flexibility, (w) reputation, (x) teaching and being able to help others, (y) God, and (z) goal setting and achievement. Additional, separate factors were expressed in chapter 4; however, these factors are due to the nature of the business that these two entrepreneurs are involved in.

Research Question 3

What are the psychological and motivational traits shared by World Athlete Entrepreneurs and Women Business Entrepreneurs.

The data accumulated concluded Women Athlete Entrepreneurs to fit closer in relation to past studies of entrepreneurial motivation than the Women Business Entrepreneurs surveyed in this particular study. The achievement characteristic is the distinguishable factor between the two groups. Women Business Entrepreneurs scored very low with the achievement factor being a motivational characteristic. The Edwards Personal Preference Schedule debated the achievement difference and confirmed an association with this characteristic. Both entrepreneur groups are in association with the motivational characteristics of (a) utilizing a skill or talent and (b) fulfilling a passion.

The chi-square test found an association of thirteen psychological characteristics between World Athlete Entrepreneurs and Women Business Entrepreneurs (a) abasement, (b) achievement, (c) affiliation, (d) aggression, (e) autonomy, (f) change, (g) dominance, (h) endurance, (i) exhibition, (j) intraception, (k) nurturance, (l) order, (m) succorance. The two groups do not have an association with the deference characteristic.

The Edwards Personal Preference Schedule challenged the achievement factor that scored lower for Women Business Entrepreneurs motivational reasons, discussed in the previous section. The chi-square test analyzing the data confirmed there is an association between both entrepreneur groups.

Research Question 4

What human and social capital factors do World Athlete Entrepreneurs and Women Business Entrepreneurs attain (age, experience, education)?

Social capital. The literature review discusses social capital as playing a significant role in entrepreneur success. This success factor continues this relation between the two entrepreneur groups of this study. Both categories submitted responses of the importance of networking and continuing education in this and other research questions. Chapter 4 explains how this social capital is utilized between the two entrepreneur groups.

Human capital. The results of this research study are in concurrence with past studies claiming age (35 years or older) to be a positive influence for success. The investigation between World Athlete Entrepreneurs and Women Business Entrepreneurs find they are in association with these past studies. World Athlete Entrepreneurs did have an equal count in the 18-25-age range and data recommends these women are successful due to having a considerable amount of experience, and family or spousal support that will be discussed later.

Human assets of education and experience differ between both entrepreneur categories regarding the pursuing of success. A high level of experience supports World Athlete Entrepreneurs in their achievement goal and Women Business Entrepreneurs are supported on their education.

It is suggested by the data analysis World Athlete Entrepreneurs take a minimum of eleven years to reach their level of success. It is presumed this is the reason why Women Athlete Entrepreneurs scored higher in the endurance psychological characteristic. Women Business Entrepreneurs reach their level at a minimum of five years. There is a significant difference in the educational level of both entrepreneurs. According to the statistics, World Athlete Entrepreneurs are commonly found to hold only high school diplomas and Women Business Entrepreneurs are commonly found to hold college education. Both entrepreneur types were equal in holding professional licenses as additional training and education.

These statistics are predicted to change in the near future as World Athlete Entrepreneurs are furthering their education in college and pursuing bachelor's degrees displayed in the data analysis charts. Observations of the professional rodeo websites containing many women barrel racer biographies affirm that these athletes are moving forward with their educational level. The barrel racers pursuing or having completed a bachelor's degree are in concurrence with past research studies suggesting that athletes are pursuing a bachelor's degree education.

Research Question 5

What kinds of financial availability do World Athlete Entrepreneurs and Women Business Entrepreneurs use during their venture?

The results from the investigation of this research study are in concurrence with past studies in regards to bootstrapping and business angels being the main financial strategies for entrepreneurs in keeping their endeavor continuing. It was pointed out in the literature review about other studies claiming insufficient evidence of discrimination in lending practices. On the other hand, it is expressed women are required to provide higher levels of credibility making it hard for her to take advantage of this particular financing availability. Data accumulated from this exploration found only three Women Business Entrepreneurs received business loans.

To illustrate the utilization of bootstrapping techniques Women Business Entrepreneurs rely on the sales of their products or services being internally generated and other personal funding such as savings and credit cards. World Athlete Entrepreneurs are similar in association as they rely on winnings and other personal funding such as savings, credit cards, and second jobs. Several World Athlete Entrepreneurs discussed the capability of receiving funds by conducting clinics and other instructional means, training, endorsements, sponsorships, product royalties, stallion breeding services, and selling barrel horses.

Research question 6

Are both women entrepreneurs employed in other disciplines for additional financing?

Research has presented many articles and documents of entrepreneurial practices in having second jobs to help in the financing, especially in the beginning stages. Some continue to hold second jobs to have the backing of financial security. A second reason is to enhance the entrepreneur's reputation and utilize his or her education such as teaching college or vocational classes. It is concluded World Athlete Entrepreneurs are closely associated with the literature and more likely to hold second jobs in helping to invest in their endeavor.

It was assumed that most of these World Athlete Entrepreneurs would be involved in a horse industry career as a second job or be self-employed. The results confirmed differently. Despite horse industry positions placing high in statistics, the findings represent World Athlete Entrepreneurs to be either self-employed, consisting of equine or other professional oriented businesses; or involved in working for professional companies with careers in engineering, medicine, executive level positions, and state officials.

World Athlete Entrepreneurs are similar in association with past entrepreneurial studies as discussed previously with having the capability of additional financing from training, teaching, and other means related to one's barrel racing career.

The results of this study; however, distinguishes past findings expressing Women Business Entrepreneurs to hold second jobs. Women Business Entrepreneurs did not place as high in practicing this type of strategy. Participants claiming to work second jobs expressed being involved with a second business or no explanation was given.

77

Research Question 7

How does the World Athlete Entrepreneur and the Women Business Entrepreneur practice the strategic art of benchmarking?

The findings present an association between World Athlete Entrepreneurs and Women Business Entrepreneurs in the utilization of benchmarking techniques. Both entrepreneurs set entrepreneurial goals, as discussed in research question 1, which is (a) financial well being, (b) self-actualization, and (c) achievement. The data analysis displays results showing that in order to reach a success level, both entrepreneur groups consistently observe and measure the competition with various practices that involves each industry such as trade publications, studying the business craft, and other continuing education methods.

Both entrepreneurs are in agreement of having a support system such as mentors or trainers for a benchmarking coadjutant. World Athlete Entrepreneurs benchmark by watching videotapes of their runs for self-improvement and continuously observe their finances. Thus, in similar significance, Women Business Entrepreneurs benchmark by observing their sales and profit reports. In addition, they continuously search for capability of keeping the overhead expenses low.

Research Question 8

Do Women Business Entrepreneurs and World Athlete Entrepreneurs experience the same barriers of (a) financial issues, (b) family, and (c) genetic stereotyping?

Financial. The data analysis presents a significant association of financial barriers between World Athlete Entrepreneurs and Women Business Entrepreneurs.

78

World Athlete Entrepreneurs expressed more detail of this barrier. The barrel racing industry has established higher expenses through the years, which has been exhibited by experience and observation. As the industry advances in new techniques to prosper, expenses have inclined in many areas such as (a) entry fees, (b) horse trailer costs, (c) cost of vehicle and the maintenance of keeping it on the road, (d) gas expense, (e) clothes and accessories, (f) purchases of barrel horses, (g) veterinarians, (h) equine chiropractic and massage therapy services, (i) equine dental services, (j) equine vitamins and supplements, (k) top equine feeding products, (l) stall management products, (m) equine tack and accessories, and n) traveling expenses such as overnight stall costs, food, and hotel for the World Athlete Entrepreneur if the trailer has no living quarters.

In relation to Women Business Entrepreneurs consistently finding ways to cut expenses, the World Athlete Entrepreneur tries to cut corners in appropriate areas but expenses are kept for the horse in order to keep it in top performing condition. The cost of horses can soar up to $70,000 for proven competitors but the average is $10,000 - $25,000. World Athlete Entrepreneurs also train their own horses so; they are purchased at younger ages and therefore, are purchased for a less significant cost. Prices vary from an average of $1,500 - $5,000. In addition, if she does not have living quarters in the trailer, alternative sleeping arrangements are made with the opportunity to either (a) set up tents, (b) set up cots in the horse accommodations of the trailer or by the stall, or (c) to sleep in the vehicle

Family. Brodsky (1993) claimed that Women Business Entrepreneurs are (a) most likely to be divorced, (b) have no family support, and (c) had to wait till the children grew to pursue their venture. The investigation of this research study presents findings

79

that are not of concurrence with this past research. The findings determine World Athlete Entrepreneurs and Women Business Entrepreneurs are married and have family support. The chi-square test proves there is an association of the two entrepreneur types in regards to marriage status. World Athlete Entrepreneurs experience higher cooperation with family support. Chi-Square tests confirmed this study not to be in concurrence with past research findings of entrepreneurs having to wait for children to grow before pursuing an endeavor. But, for this particular study, the chi-square analysis confirmed an association between World Athlete Entrepreneurs and Women Business Entrepreneurs. An additional discovery analyzed by a chi-square test, accepted the null hypothesis for confirming there is not an association between World Athlete Entrepreneurs and Women Business Entrepreneurs on the number of children women have. World Athlete Entrepreneurs are less compatible with raising children.

Genetic Stereotyping. Society remains stringent about women wanting to succeed in a man's world and this is proven in the business and athletic arena. Catley and Hamilton's (1998) study are examples stating women lack the characteristics so they remain less successful. Others have debated these studies such as Kalleberg and Leicht, 1991, included in the study by Catley and Hamilton .

This research study confirms there is an association of genetic stereotyping experienced between Women Business Entrepreneurs and World Athlete Entrepreneurs such as (a) the experience of higher expectations and (b) not being allowed to communicate with the male network to do the appropriate business. An astonishing factor found to be experienced is the negativity of other women.

Additional barriers. Additional impediments experienced by both World Athlete Entrepreneurs and Woman Business Entrepreneurs were discussed in chapter 4. The common factors constructed for both entrepreneurs are (a) time management, (b) health and disability issues, (c) balancing the venture with family, (d) working for self or others, and (e) college.

Research question 9

Do World Athlete Entrepreneurs and Women Business Entrepreneurs share in the same Birth Theory or in the Only or Eldest daughter Syndrome?

The literature review discusses research debating whether entrepreneurs are from families with an entrepreneurial background called the Birth Theory. The argument stressed throughout research is whether a person inherits entrepreneurial traits or taught. The family background resulted in a significant relation because the data analysis confirms both World Athlete Entrepreneurs and Women Business Entrepreneurs are from families with similar background. This also suggests the reason for supportive families discussed in earlier results.

An additional characteristic discussed in the literature review, is the theory that Women Business Entrepreneurs are only or eldest daughters known as the Only or Eldest Daughter Syndrome. The chi-square tests analyzed the data retrieved and the results were not of concurrence with other past findings exemplifying the Only or Eldest Daughter Theory *not* to be true. However, for this particular study, it is confirmed there is an association between World Athlete Entrepreneurs and Women Business Entrepreneurs of *not* being an eldest or only daughter.

81

Summary

The objective of this study was to explore and compare World Athlete Entrepreneurs to see if there was an association with Women Business Entrepreneurs. Nine questions navigated the study to find associations (a) are Women Business Entrepreneurs and World Athlete Entrepreneurs successful, (b) how do Women Business Entrepreneurs and World Athlete Entrepreneurs measure success, (c) what are the psychological and motivational traits shared by World Athlete Entrepreneurs and Woman Business Entrepreneurs, (d) what human and social capital factors do World Athlete Entrepreneurs and Women Business Entrepreneurs attain (e.g. age, experience, education), (e) what kind of financial availability do World Athlete Entrepreneurs use during their venture, (f) are both women entrepreneurs employed in other disciplines for additional financing, (g) how do World Athlete Entrepreneurs and Women Business Entrepreneurs practice the strategic art of benchmarking, (h) do Women Business Entrepreneurs and World Athlete Entrepreneurs experience the same barriers of financial issues, family, and genetic stereotyping, and (i) do World Athlete Entrepreneurs and Women Business Entrepreneurs share in the same Birth Theory or Only or Eldest Daughter Syndrome?

The results of this study confirmed the association between World Athlete Entrepreneurs and Women Business Entrepreneurs with the statement in the introduction that identifies entrepreneurship as (a) fulfilling a passion, (b) utilizing skills and talents, and (c) the needing of high achievement. Success is defined differently for each individual participant but the data shows there is an association between World Athlete Entrepreneurs and Women Business Entrepreneurs in relation with characteristics to the entrepreneur definition of pursuing (a) financial well being, (b) self-actualization, and (c) achievement. The associations of psychological and motivational characteristics are also found between the two groups investigated in accordance with the Edwards Personal Preference Schedule.

Previous research studies found social and human capital to be of significant value for an entrepreneur. This study found World Athlete Entrepreneurs and Women Business Entrepreneurs to be in concurrence with the association of age (35 years or older) being a positive influence. Both entrepreneurs express that social capital is important and networking is a big contributor in both industries. Additional human capital factors such as experience and education differ. World Athlete Entrepreneur's level of success is determined by the years of experience and education determines the level of success for the Women Business Entrepreneur.

The business strategies practiced by both types of entrepreneurs are significantly associated. Financial strategies conducted in order to continue their endeavor is associated with bootstrapping techniques and business angels. World Athlete Entrepreneurs are more likely to hold second jobs for additional financing of their venture. Benchmarking practices are similar in that they both use (a) continuous education, (b) trainers or mentors, and (c) data analysis to consistently measure objectives in the pursuit of reaching their success level.

Past research studies discuss the three main barriers for women entrepreneurs and they are (a) financial issues, (b) family issues, and (c) genetic stereotyping. The exploration of this study confirms the association of World Athlete Entrepreneurs and Women Business Entrepreneurs with financial barriers and genetic stereotyping with the past research conducted. It further proved an association with this particular investigation. However, no association is found between the two entrepreneurs explored in this study with the family barrier because they are found to have family support. For this study there is an association between the two entrepreneurs.

The final theory investigated for this exploratory, comparative analysis was to investigate the Birth Theory and the Only or Eldest Daughter Syndrome. There is an association between World Athlete Entrepreneurs and Women Business Entrepreneurs being from families with related backgrounds. World Athlete Entrepreneurs are from families with rodeo or some horse industry background. Women Business Entrepreneurs are from entrepreneurial families having owned or owns a business.

The investigation of this study rejects the Only or Eldest Daughter Syndrome theory and finds no association with past research. The results from this study; however, confirms an association between the two types of entrepreneurs *not* being only or eldest daughters.

Recommendations

The results of this investigation display a positive association between World Athlete Entrepreneurs and Women Business Entrepreneurs with the entrepreneur definition pronounced in this study. Based on the findings of this study, recommendations are offered to (a) society and business professionals, (b) World Athlete Entrepreneurs, and (c) Researchers.

Recommendations for Society and Business Professionals

The association of business strategic practices presents sufficient evidence to change the negative perceptions about this elite World Athlete Entrepreneur. The data concludes that barrel racers are professional athletes and pursue the same financial gain as other professional athletes and business entrepreneurs. In fact, it is experienced and observed that World Athlete Entrepreneurs have a greater opportunity to experience higher investment in pursuit of a projected financial gain. Therefore, many do need sponsorships and endorsements in order to help with their financing so they can do what they do best.

Literature expresses that businesses seek athletes for sponsorship that will represent their company well and will have a high response rate. The horse industry in itself is a billion dollar industry providing many jobs or career positions. Rodeo is proven to be one of the top spectator sports. Statistics show spectators are from high to middle class income families. The rodeo arena consists of many reputable sponsors such as MBNA financial services and other Bank institutions, Wrangler, Levis, Coca-Cola, John-Deere, and Dodge Truck.

It is highly recommended for businesses to sponsor or endorse women barrel racers.

Recommendation for World Athlete Entrepreneurs

The findings of this study are presented as an additional networking source. Various insights of strategic business practices are expressed that can be utilized for benchmarking practices.

Recommendations for Researchers

The constructs of finding an association between World Athlete Entrepreneurs and Women Business Entrepreneurs were found in this study. Research defining the actual financial comparisons of both entrepreneur types should be conducted in order to give a visual presentation of the actual financial opportunities women barrel racers have and to compare the financial outlay in comparison of Women Business Entrepreneurs. This may shed light on the reasoning of women barrel racers to be more likely of holding second jobs. Does it hold a higher investment cost?

World Athlete Entrepreneurs are now pursuing or having completed bachelor's degrees and other college education. A research study should be performed of the financial status between women barrel racers holding a college education versus women barrel racers with only a high school diploma. Are there advantages for having a college education in the barrel racing industry?

Genetic stereotyping is found to be experienced by both entrepreneur categories. A review of past studies found one conducted in the 1970's that found men to be more competitive with women than male counterparts. Research defining this theory should be conducted to see if it still holds true in present time and to find the rationale behind it.

Financial impediments are experienced and literature claims women are not discriminated against in seeking business loans. However, they are held with higher expectations of credibility. Research should be performed in the area of (a) finding out the actual business loans given for women and (b) the factors that make it more stringent for them in comparison of men.

Sponsorships and endorsements are expressed as a financial boost throughout this research study. Research should be conducted to find the percentage rate of the actual contribution it gives on the road to success.

REFERENCES

Anonymous (1995). The key to female entrepreneurial success-born not made-new research claims. *Women in Management Review, 10*(4), 33.

Baron, R.A., & Markman, G.D. (2000). Beyond social capital: How social skills can enhance entrepreneurs' success. *The Academy of Management Executive, 14*(1), 106-117.

Beugelsdijk, S., & Noorderhaven, N. (2005). Personality characteristics of self-employed: An empirical study. *Small Business Economics, 24,* 159-167.

Birley, S. (1989). Female Entrepreneurs: Are they really different? *Journal of Small Business Management, 32-37.*

Blanchflower, D.G., & Oswald, A.J. (1998). What makes an entrepreneur? *Journal or Labor Economics, 16(1),* 26-60.

Brodsky, M.A. (1993). Successful female corporate managers and entrepreneurs. *Group & Organization Management, 18*(3), 366-37.

Bruni, A., Gherardi, S., Poggio, B., (2004). Entrepreneur-mentality, gender and the study of women entrepreneurs. *Journal of Organizational Change Management, 17*(3), 256.

Buttner, E.H., & Rosen, B.H. (1989). Funding new business ventures: Are decision-makers biased against women entrepreneurs? *Journal of Business Venturing, 4*(4), 249-261.

Caird, S.P. (1993). What do psychological tests suggest about entrepreneurs? *Journal of Managerial Psychology, 8*(6), 11-21.

Carter, N.M., Brush, C.G., Greene, P.G., Gatewood, E., & Hart, M.M. (2003). Women entrepreneurs who break through to equity financing: The influence of human, social, and financial capital. *Venture Capital, 5*(1), 1-28.

Catley, S., Hamilton, R.T. (1998). Small business development and gender of owner. *The Journal of Management Development, 17*(1), 75.

Cooper, D.R., & Schindler, P.S. (2001). *Business Research Methods* (7th ed.). Boston: McGraw-Hill.

Creswell, J.W. (1994). Research Design: Qualitative & quantitative approaches. Thousand Oaks, CA: Sage.

Creswell, J.W. (1998). Qualitative inquiry and research designs: Choosing among five traditions. Thousand Oaks, CA: Sage.

Creswell, J.W. (2002). Educational research: Planning, conducting, and evaluating quantitative and qualitative research. Upper Saddle River, NJ: Merrill Prentice Hall.

Crompton, J.L. (2004). Conceptualization and alternate operationalizations of the Measurement of sponsorship effectiveness in sport. Leisure Studies, 23(3), 267-281.

Danco, L.A. (1993). Something out of nothing. Agency Sales, 23(10), 30-36.

Daneshvary, R., & Schwer, R.K. (2000). The association endorsement and consumers' intention to purchase. The Journal of Consumer Marketing, 17(3), 203.

DePaula, M. (2003). Business owners are putting out with plastic. *US Banker, 113*(8), 54.

De Vries, M.F.R. Ket (1996). The anatomy of the entrepreneur. *Human Relations, 49*(7), 853- 884.

Edwards, A.L. (1953). *Edwards Personal Preference Schedule.* New York: The Psychological Corporation.

Garrett, S. (2006, May). The true entrepreneur: Most people work for themselves to make more money and have more control, but being a successful entrepreneur involves a lot more. *Financial Planning, 36*(5), 115-116.

Gray, P.B. (2004, August). Queen of the rodeo: An ex-teacher learns to be a rising star of barrel racing. *Fortune,* September 2004, Retrieved on November 3, 2005 from www.fortune.com.

Hatala, J.P. (2005). Identifying barriers to self-employment: The development and validation of the barriers to entrepreneurship tool. *Performance Improvement Quarterly, 18*(4), 50-71.

Hickman, T.M., Lawrence, K.E., & Ward, J.C. (2005). A social identities perspective on the effects of corporate sport sponsorship on employees. *Sport Marketing Quarterly, 14*(3), 148-158.

Hormozi, A.M. (2004). Becoming an entrepreneur: How to start a small business. *International Journal of Management, 21*(3), 278-286.

Hunter, R.J., & Mayo, A.M. (1999, June/September). The business of sport: The mid-atlantic. *Journal of Business, 35*(2/3), 75-77.

Kom, D.J. (2005, February). Finding cash for your business. *Black Enterprise, 35*(7), 82-88.

Llewellyn, D.J., & Wilson, K. (2003). The controversial role of personality traits in entrepreneurial psychology. *Education & Training, 45*(6), 341-146.

Madsen, H., & Neergaard, H., Ulhoi, J.P.(2003). Knowledge-intensive entrepreneurship and human capital. *Journal of Small Business and Enterprise Development, 10* (4), 426-435.

McFarland, K. (2005, November). The psychology of success. *Inc., 27*(11), 158-160.

Mittelstaedt, J.D., Riesz, P.C., & Burns, WJ. (2000). Why are endorsements effective? Sortingamong theories of product and endorser effects. *Journal of Current Issues and Research in Advertising, 22*(1).

Morgan, G. (1997). *Images of organization (*2nd ed.). London: Sage.

Morris, M.H., Miyasaki, N.N., Walters, C.E., & Coombes, S.M. (2006). The dilemma of growth: understanding venture size choices of women entrepreneurs. *Journal of Small Business Management, 44*(2), 221-245.

Neck, C.P., Neck, H.M., Manz, C.C., & Godwin, J. (1999). "I think I can; I think I can" a self-leadership perspective toward enhancing entrepreneur thought patterns, self-efficacy, and performance. *Journal of Managerial Psychology, 14*(6), 477.

Parker, O., & Kovacs, N. (2001). The benchmarking advantage: A benefit management tool. *Canadian HR Reporter, 14*(12), 10-12.

Pearson, D.W., & Haney, C.A. (1999, August). The rodeo cowboy: Cultural icon, athlete, or entrepreneur? *Journal of Sport & Social Issues, 23*(3), 308-327.

Robinson, K.M. (1999). *Finding the lost story of the cowgirls.* Published master's theses, Ohio State University, Ohio.

Sage, G. (1993). Entrepreneurship as an economic development strategy. *Economic Development Review, 11*(2), 66-68.

Skelton, L.M. (2006). Female Entrepreneurs, work-family conflict, and venture performance: new insights into the work-family interface. *Journal of Small Business Management, 44*(2), 285-298.

Shank, G., & Villella, O. (2004). Building on new foundations: Core principles and new directions for qualitative research. *The Journal of Educational Research, 98*(1), 46-56.

Sorheim, R. (2005). Business angels as facilitators for further finance: An exploratory study. *Journal of Small Business and Enterprise Development, 12*(2), 178-192.

Teal, E.J., Carroll, A.B. (1999). Moral reasoning skills: Are entrepreneurs different? *Journal of Business Ethics, 19*(3), 229-241.

Tellis, W. (1997). Application of a case study methodology. *The Qualitative   Report, 3*(3).   Retrieved on September 3, 2006 from http://www.nova.edu/ssss/QR/QR-3/tellis2.html.

Thompson, J.L. (1999). The world of the entrepreneur: A new perspective. *Journal of Workplace Learning, 11*(6).

VanGilderen, M., Thurik, R., & Bosma, N. (2005). Success and risk factors in the pre-startup phase. *Small Business Economics, 25,* 365-380.

Virtanen, M. (nd). The role of different theories in explaining entrepreneurship. *Helsinki School of Economics and Business Administration, Small Business Center: Finland.* Retrieved 3/13/04 at http://www.sbaer.uca.edu/Research/1997/ ICSB/ 97ICS009.htm.

Winn, J. (2004). Entrepreneurship: Not an easy path to top management for women. *Women in Management Review, 19*(3), 143.

Woldt, L. C. (2005, June). Business success: Entrepreneurial visions from the early stage. *Dissertation Abstracts International, 66* (07), 183. (UMI No. AAT3181093).

DATA COLLECTION INSTRUMENT – WAE QUESTIONNAIRE

Questionnaire for World Athlete Entrepreneurs (Barrel Racers)

1. Why did you start barrel racing? (Can choose more than one)
    a. High need for achievement
    b. Change
    c. Dominance
    d. Flexibility
    e. To utilize a skill or talent
    f. To gain a sense of self
    g. To gain Confidence
    h. To fulfill a passion

2. What is your age?
    a. 18-25
    b. 26-31
    c. 32 – 38
    d. 39 – 44
    e. 45 – 50
    f. 51 – 56
    g. 57 +

3. How long have you been barrel racing?
    a. under 5 years
    b. 5 – 10 years
    c. 11- 15 years
    d. 16 – 20 years
    e. 21 - 25 years
    f. 26 – 30 years

4. What is your highest educational level?

    a. high school
    b. GED
    c. Associate of Arts or Associate of Science degree
    d. Bachelor's degree
    e. Master's degree
    f. PhD
    g. Working on or received another type of professional degree or license

5. How do you finance your venture?

6. Is another job held? Please state what your second job is?
   a. Yes
   b. No

7. How do you utilize benchmarking?

8. What is your marital status?
   a. Single
   b. Married
   c. Separated
   d. Divorced

9. Do you have family and/or spousal support with your venture?

10. Are there any other barriers you experience while traveling to your goal of success? If so, what are they?

11. How many children do you have?

12. If have children, did you have to wait till your children were older before pushing a successful endeavor?

    a. Yes
    b. No
    c. Not applicable

13. Are you an only child?
    a. Yes
    b. No

14. Are you an eldest child?
    a. Yes
    b. No

15. Are you from a rodeo or another type of horse-oriented family?

    a. Yes
    b. No

16. What are the factors or characteristics that you feel determine your success?

17. If the answer to question 9 is no, what are the major factors that contribute to the reasons why? If you would rather not answer this question write "No answer". If this does not apply to you write "N/A".

APPENDIX B.

DATA COLLECTION INSTRUMENT – WBE QUESTIONNAIRE

Questionnaire for Women Business Entrepreneurs

1. Why did you start your own business? (can choose more than one)
   a. High need for achievement
   b. Change
   c. Dominance
   d. Flexibility
   e. To utilize a skill or talent
   f. To gain a sense of self
   g. To gain Confidence
   h. To fulfill a passion

2. What is your age?
   a. 18-25
   b. 26-31
   c. 32 – 38
   d. 39 – 44
   e .45 – 50
   f. 51 – 56
   g. 57 +

3. How long have you owned your own business?
   a. under 5 years
   b. 5 – 10 years
   c. 11- 15 years
   d. 16 – 20 years
   e. 21 - 25 years
   f. 26 – 30 years

4. What is your highest educational level?

      a. high school
      b. GED
      c. Associate of Arts or Associate of Science degree
      d. Bachelor's degree
      e. Master's degree
      f. PhD
      g. Working on or received another type of professional degree or license

5. How do you finance your venture?

6. Is another job held? Please state what your second job is?
      a. Yes
        b. No

7. How do you utilize benchmarking?

8. What is your marital status?
      a. Single
      b. Married
      c. Separated
      d.Divorced

9. Do you have family and/or spousal support with your endeavor?

10. Are there any other barriers you experience while traveling to your goal of success? If so, what are they?

11. How many children do you have?

12. If have children, did you have to wait till your children were older before pushing a successful endeavor?

       a. Yes
       b. No
       c. Not applicable

13. Are you an only child?
       a. Yes
       b. No

14. Are you an eldest child?
       a. Yes
       b. No

15. Are you from a business entrepreneurial family (one that owns or has owned a business)?
       a. Yes
       b. No

16. What are the factors or characteristics that you feel determine your success?

17. If the answer to question 9 is no, what are the major factors that contribute to the reasons why? If you would rather not answer this question write "No answer". If this does not apply to you write "N/A".

APPENDIX C.

INFORMED CONSENT LETTER

CAPELLA UNIVERSITY
225 South 6th Street, 9th Floor
Minneapolis, MN 55402

INFORMED CONSENT DOCUMENT

You are being asked to participate in a research study designed for the completion of doctoral studies by Melissa L. Greer, ABD who resides in ███████████████.

The purpose of this study is to compare and contrast World Athlete Entrepreneurs (women barrel racers) with Women Business Entrepreneurs and determine if there is an alignment between women who race and women who have their own businesses. This study is to help a) enhance cultural education and prevent further criticisms (b) educate World-Athlete Entrepreneurs on these findings; (c) help the World Athlete Entrepreneur build a business strategy; and (d) educate business owners and corporations about this environment in hopes of giving a positive enlightenment about this growing industry. By providing this knowledge, it is further hoped that corporations and individual decision-makers will receive a positive reaction about the business tactics of World Athlete Entrepreneurs and enhance decision-making authority for sponsorship and endorsement decisions.

The title of this research study is "The World Athlete Entrepreneur Burning the Barrel for Business Endeavors: A Comparison and Contrast Research Study of women who barrel race and women who own their own businesses. The reason you have been selected to participate in this study is that you meet the requirements needed to pursue the data. The requirement of this study targets a minimum sample of thirty World Athlete Entrepreneurs (barrel racers) and thirty Women Business Entrepreneurs. The World Athlete Entrepreneur must compete at a minimum of 40 rodeos or barrel racing events a year and earn a gross profit. The Women Business Entrepreneur must meet the requirement of having been in business for at least one year and make a profit. The World Athlete Entrepreneur (barrel racer) and the Woman Business Entrepreneur must meet the minimum age requirement of 18 years old.

The completion of a questionnaire that entails the business strategies and impediments of your business endeavor is needed along with the completion of the Edwards Personal Preference Schedule. This test will analyze the psychological and motivational characteristics of your job title.

The length of time allocated for the completion of these questionnaires should take no longer than one hour. No personal information is asked (such as name, address, or phone number) to be displayed on the questionnaires or other written material recorded for this research study. This is in order for the participants to remain autonomous. The researcher, doctoral committee, supervisor, or the Institutional Review Board may inspect data obtained as a result of your participation. Once all data is analyzed, combined, and given a result, the information is displayed. There are no foreseen risks to the participants of this study because no personal information is asked on the questionnaires that will designate whom the data belongs to. Participants are treated with respect and in an ethical manner.

Participation in this study is strictly voluntary. There will not be any negative consequences if participation is withdrawn from the study. In addition, the researcher, without prior notice or consent, may terminate participation if it is found that the participant does not meet the requirements needed for the study.

The following information is the authorized representatives that can be contacted if there should be any questions or concerns:

Melissa L. Greer, ABD, Researcher

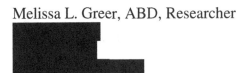

Dr. Joe LeVesque, Research Supervisor

Dr. Karen Viechnicki

A copy of this Informed Consent Document will be given to the participant for their records.

I have read and understood this consent form. I understand that participation is strictly voluntary and I am under no obligation to contribute to this study. I understand that I will receive a copy of this consent form.

Participant Name   _____
                              (Printed or Typed)

                Date   _____

Participant Signature   _____

                Date   _____

APPENDIX D.

RECRUITMENT INFORMATION

Notice advertised on the Florida Equine Athlete website and the Florida Equine Athlete publication

Calling Barrel Racers and Women Business Entrepreneurs. Many of you already know that I have been working on the dissertation proposal for my doctorate degree. It has been approved and it is now time to start the gathering of data. I need YOU! The population sample needed is: 30 Barrel Racers and 30 Women Business Entrepreneurs. My dissertation is a comparison and contrast study between world athlete entrepreneurs (female barrel racers) and women business entrepreneurs to see if there is a relationship between women who race and women who own their own businesses.

The requirements to participate in this study are:

World Athlete Entrepreneurs (Barrel Racers)	Women Business Entrepreneurs
Must be female	Same
Must be 18-75 years of age	Must be of 18 – 75 years of age
Compete in at least 40 barrel races or rodeos per year	Must have owned business for at least one year
Make a gross profit not the net (meaning have made a paycheck from winnings – period).	Make a gross profit

The reasons this study is being conducted is not only to complete my doctorate degree but to (a) enhance cultural education; (b) educate world athlete entrepreneurs on these findings; (c) help the world athlete entrepreneur build a business strategy; and d) educate business owners and corporations about our environment in hopes of giving a positive enlightenment about our growing industry. By providing this knowledge, it is further hoped that corporations and individual decision-makers will receive a positive reaction about the business tactics of world athlete entrepreneurs and enhance decision-making authority for sponsorship and endorsement decisions.

BECOME A VALUABLE ASSET TO THIS STUDY!

If you meet the requirements and would like to be a part it, please contact Melissa Greer (ASAP) ████████████████████

APPENDIX E.

ACHIEVEMENT VARIABLE CHI – SQUARE TEST

	Value	df	Asymp. Sig. (2-sided)	Exact (2-sided)	Exact (1-sided)
Pearson Chi-Square	2.00[b]	1	.15		
Continuity[a]	.00	1	1.00		
Likelihood Ratio	2.77	1	.096		
Fisher's Exact Test				1.00	.500
N of Valid	2				

Note. Computed only for a 2x2 table

Note. 4 cells (100.0%) have expected count less than 5. The minimum expected count is .50.

APPENDIX F.

CHANGE VARIABLE CHI-SQUARE TEST

	Value	df	Asymp. (2-sided)	Exact (2-sided)	Exact (1-sided)
Pearson chi-square	2.000[b]	1	.157		
Continuity Correction[a]	.000	1	1.000		
Likelihood Ratio	2.773	1	.096		
Fisher's Exact Test				1.000	.500
N of Valid	2				

Note. Computed only for a 2x2 table

Note. 4 cells (100.0%) have expected count less than 5. The minimum expected count is .50.

APPENDIX G.

CONFIDENCE CHI-SQUARE TEST

The confidence chi-square test had a one participant in each category that claimed the confidence variable as a type of motivational characteristic.

	Value
Pearson chi-square	2 .[a]
N of Valid Cases	

Note. No statistics are computed because CONFIDEN is a constant.

APPENDIX H.

DOMINANCE VARIABLE CHI – SQUARE TEST

	Value	df	Asymp. (2-sided)	Exact (2-sided)	Exact (1-sided)
Pearson chi-square	2.00 [b]	1	.157		
Continuity Correction	.000	1	1.00		
Likelihood	2.77	1	.096		
Fisher's Exact Test				1.00	.500
N of Valid Cases	2				

Note. Computed only for a 2x2 table

Note. 4 cells (100.0%) have expected count less than 5. The minimum expected count is .50.

APPENDIX I.

FLEXIBILITY VARIABLE CHI-SQUARE TEST

	Value	df	Asymp. Sig. (2-sided)	Exact Sig. (2-sided)	Exact Sig. (1-sided)
Pearson chi-square	2.00 [b]	1	.157		
Continuity Correction	.000	1	1.00		
Likelihood Ratio	2.77	1	.096		
Fisher's Exact Test				1.00	.500
N of Valid Cases	2				

Note. Computed only for a 2x2 table

Note. 4 cells (100.0%) have expected count less than 5. The minimum expected count is .50.

APPENDIX J.

TO FULFILL A PASSION VARIABLE CHI – SQUARE TEST

	Value	df	Asymp. Sig. (2-sided)	Exact Sig. (2-sided)	Exact Sig. (1-sided)
Pearson chi-square	2.000[b]	1	.157		
Continuity Correction[a]	.000	1	1.000		
Likelihood Ratio	2.773	1	.096		
Fisher's Exact Test				1.000	.500
N of Valid Cases	2				

Note. Computed only for a 2x2 table

Note. 4 cells (100.0%) have expected count less than 5. The minimum expected count is .50.

107

APPENDIX K.

SENSE OF SELF-VARIABLE CHI-SQUARE TEST

	Value	df	Asymp. Sig. (2-sided)	Exact Sig. (2-sided)	Exact Sig. (1-sided)
Pearson Chi-Square	2.000[b]	1	.157		
Continuity Correction	.000	1	1.000		
Likelihood Ratio	2.773	1	.096		
Fisher's Exact Test				1.000	.500
N of Valid Cases	2				

Note. Computed only for a 2x2 table

Note. 4 cells (100.0%) have expected count less than 5. The minimum expected count is .50.

APPENDIX L.

ABILITY TO UTILIZE A SKILL OR TALENT CHI-SQUARE TEST

	Value	df	Asymp. Sig (2-sided)	Exact Sig. (2-sided)	Exact Sig (1-sided)
Pearson Chi-Square	2.00 [b]	1	.15		
Continuity Correction	.00	1	1.00		
Likelihood Ratio	2.77	1	.09		
Fisher's Exact				1.00	.50
N of Valid	2				

Note. Computed only for a 2x2 table

Note. 4 cells (100.0%) have expected count less than 5. The minimum
Expected count is .50.

APPENDIX M.

MARITAL STATUS CHI-SQUARE TESTS - MARRIED VARIABLE

	Value	df	Asymp. Sig. (2-sided)	Exact Sig. (2-sided)	Exact Sig. (1-sided)
Pearson Chi-Square	2.00 [b]	1	.157		
Continuity Correction	.000	1	1.00		
Likelihood Ratio	2.77	1	.096		
Fisher's Exact Test				1.00	.500
N of Valid Cases	2				

Note. Computed only for a 2x2 table

Note. 4 cells (100.0%) have expected count less than 5. The minimum expected count is .50

APPENDIX N.

MARITAL STATUS CHI-SQUARE TESTS - DIVORCED VARIABLE

	Value	df	Asymp. (2-sided)	Exact (2-sided)	Exact (1-sided)
Pearson chi-square	2.00 [b]	1	.157		
Continuity Correction	.000	1	1.00		
Likelihood Ratio	2.77	1	.096		
Fisher's Exact Test				1.00	.500
N of Valid Cases	2				

Note. Computed only for a 2x2

Note. 4 cells (100.0%) have expected count less than 5. The minimum expected count is .50.

APPENDIX O.

MARITAL STATUS CHI-SQUARE TESTS - SEPARATED VARIABLE

	Value	df	Asymp. Sig. (2-sided)	Exact Sig. (2-sided)	Exact Sig. (1-sided)
Pearson Chi-Square	2.000[b]	1	.157		
Continuity Correction	.000	1	1.000		
Likelihood Ratio	2.773	1	.096		
Fisher's Exact Test				1.000	.500
N of Valid Cases	2				

Note. Computed only for a 2x2 table

Note. 4 cells (100.0%) have expected count less than 5. The minimum expected count is .50.

APPENDIX P.

MARITAL STATUS CHI-SQUARE TESTS - SINGLE VARIABLE

	Value	df	Asymp. Sig. (2-sided)	Exact Sig. (2-sided)	Exact Sig. (1-sided)
Pearson chi-square	2.000[b]	1	.157		
Continuity Correction	.000	1	1.000		
Likelihood Ratio	2.773	1	.096		
Fisher's Exact Test				1.000	.500
N of Valid Cases	2				

Note. Computed only for a 2x2 table

Note. 4 cells (100.0%) have expected count less than 5. The minimum expected count is .50.

APPENDIX Q.

EPPS PSYCHOLOGICAL CHARACTERISTICS CROSS TABULATIONS - ABASEMENT VARIABLE

| | | ENTTYPE | | | | | |
| | | 1 | | 2 | | Total | |
		Count	% within Abasement	Count	% within Abasement	Count	% within Abasement
Abasement	5			1	100.0%	1	100.0%
	7			1	100.0%	1	100.0%
	8			2	100.0%	2	100.0%
	9			2	100.0%	2	100.0%
	10	3	60.0%	2	40.0%	5	100.0%
	11	1	25.0%	3	75.0%	4	100.0%
	12	5	71.4%	2	28.6%	7	100.0%
	13			2	100.0%	2	100.0%
	14	3	60.0%	2	40.0%	5	100.0%
	15	3	100.0%			3	100.0%
	16	3	60.0%	2	40.0%	5	100.0%
	17			4	100.0%	4	100.0%
	18	1	100.0%			1	100.0%
	19	1	100.0%			1	100.0%
	20	2	66.7%	1	33.3%	3	100.0%
	21	1	100.0%			1	100.0%
	23			1	100.0%	1	100.0%
	25	2	100.0%			2	100.0%
Total		25	50.0%	25	50.0%	50	100.0%

114

APPENDIX R.

EPPS PSYCHOLOGICAL CHARACTERISTICS CROSS TABULATIONS - ACHIEVEMENT VARIABLE

| | | ENTTYPE | | | | Total | |
| | | 1 | | 2 | | | |
		Count	% within Achievement	Count	% within Achievement	Count	% within Achievement
Achievement	4	1	100.0%			1	100.0%
	7	1	100.0%			1	100.0%
	8	1	100.0%			1	100.0%
	9	2	66.7%	1	33.3%	3	100.0%
	11	2	100.0%			2	100.0%
	12	1	50.0%	1	50.0%	2	100.0%
	13	2	33.3%	4	66.7%	6	100.0%
	14	2	66.7%	1	33.3%	3	100.0%
	15			3	100.0%	3	100.0%
	16	2	33.3%	4	66.7%	6	100.0%
	17	2	25.0%	6	75.0%	8	100.0%
	18	3	60.0%	2	40.0%	5	100.0%
	19	1	50.0%	1	50.0%	2	100.0%
	20	2	100.0%			2	100.0%
	21	1	100.0%			1	100.0%
	22	1	100.0%			1	100.0%
	23			1	100.0%	1	100.0%
	24	1	100.0%			1	100.0%
	26			1	100.0%	1	100.0%
Total		25	50.0%	25	50.0%	50	100.0%

APPENDIX S.

EPPS PSYCHOLOGICAL CHARACTERISTICS CROSS
TABULATION - AFFILIATION VARIABLE

		ENTTYPE					
		1		2		Total	
		Count	% within Affiliation	Count	% within Affiliation	Count	% within Affiliation
Affiliation	4	1	100.0%			1	100.0%
	6			1	100.0%	1	100.0%
	7			1	100.0%	1	100.0%
	8			1	100.0%	1	100.0%
	9	1	50.0%	1	50.0%	2	100.0%
	10	1	100.0%			1	100.0%
	11	3	75.0%	1	25.0%	4	100.0%
	12	2	50.0%	2	50.0%	4	100.0%
	13	4	80.0%	1	20.0%	5	100.0%
	14	2	100.0%			2	100.0%
	15	1	33.3%	2	66.7%	3	100.0%
	16	2	40.0%	3	60.0%	5	100.0%
	17	1	20.0%	4	80.0%	5	100.0%
	18	4	80.0%	1	20.0%	5	100.0%
	19	3	60.0%	2	40.0%	5	100.0%
	20			2	100.0%	2	100.0%
	21			1	100.0%	1	100.0%
	22			1	100.0%	1	100.0%
	23			1	100.0%	1	100.0%
Total		25	50.0%	25	50.0%	50	100.0%

116

EPPS PSYCHOLOGICAL CHARACTERISTICS CROSS TABULATION - AGGRESSION VARIABLE

		ENTTYPE				Total	
		1		2			
		Count	% within Aggression	Count	% within Aggression	Count	% within Aggression
Aggression	1			1	100.0%	1	100.0%
	2	1	100.0%			1	100.0%
	3	2	100.0%			2	100.0%
	4	1	100.0%			1	100.0%
	5	1	50.0%	1	50.0%	2	100.0%
	6	2	66.7%	1	33.3%	3	100.0%
	7	1	50.0%	1	50.0%	2	100.0%
	8	1	50.0%	1	50.0%	2	100.0%
	9	4	80.0%	1	20.0%	5	100.0%
	10	1	20.0%	4	80.0%	5	100.0%
	11	2	40.0%	3	60.0%	5	100.0%
	12	1	100.0%			1	100.0%
	13	2	40.0%	3	60.0%	5	100.0%
	14			3	100.0%	3	100.0%
	15	2	66.7%	1	33.3%	3	100.0%
	16	1	33.3%	2	66.7%	3	100.0%
	17			1	100.0%	1	100.0%
	18	1	50.0%	1	50.0%	2	100.0%
	19	1	100.0%			1	100.0%
	21	1	50.0%	1	50.0%	2	100.0%
Total		25	50.0%	25	50.0%	50	100.0%

APPENDIX U.

EPPS PSYCHOLOGICAL CHARACTERISTICS CROSS TABULATION - AUTONOMY VARIABLE

		ENTTYPE				Total	
		1		2			
		Count	% within Autonomy	Count	% within Autonomy	Count	% within Autonomy
Autonomy	4	1	100.0			1	100.0
	6	2	100.0			2	100.0
	7			1	100.0	1	100.0
	8	1	50.0	1	50.0	2	100.0
	9	3	100.0			3	100.0
	10	2	50.0	2	50.0	4	100.0
	11	3	75.0	1	25.0	4	100.0
	12	2	66.7	1	33.3	3	100.0
	13	2	100.0			2	100.0
	14	2	33.3	4	66.7	6	100.0
	15	2	40.0	3	60.0	5	100.0
	16	2	33.3	4	66.7	6	100.0
	17			2	100.0	2	100.0
	18			2	100.0	2	100.0
	19	1	33.3	2	66.7	3	100.0
	20	1	50.0	1	50.0	2	100.0
	21	1	100.0			1	100.0
	25			1	100.0	1	100.0
Total		25	50.0%	25	50.0%	50	100.0%

APPENDIX V.

EPPS PSYCHOLOGICAL CHARACTERISTICS CROSS TABULATION - CHANGE VARIABLE

| | | ENTTYPE | | | | Total | |
| | | 1 | | 2 | | | |
		Count	% within Change	Count	% within Change	Count	% within Change
Change	4	1	100.0%			1	100.0%
	5	1	100.0%			1	100.0%
	6	1	100.0%			1	100.0%
	8	3	100.0%			3	100.0%
	9	1	100.0%			1	100.0%
	10			1	100.0%	1	100.0%
	11	1	50.0%	1	50.0%	2	100.0%
	12	2	40.0%	3	60.0%	5	100.0%
	13	3	60.0%	2	40.0%	5	100.0%
	14			4	100.0%	4	100.0%
	15	2	50.0%	2	50.0%	4	100.0%
	17	1	33.3%	2	66.7%	3	100.0%
	18	3	60.0%	2	40.0%	5	100.0%
	19	3	75.0%	1	25.0%	4	100.0%
	20			2	100.0%	2	100.0%
	21			1	100.0%	1	100.0%
	22			1	100.0%	1	100.0%
	23	2	40.0%	3	60.0%	5	100.0%
	27	1	100.0%			1	100.0%
Total		25	50.0%	25	50.0%	50	100.0%

APPENDIX W.

EPPS PSYCHOLOGICAL CHARACTERISTICS CROSS TABULATION - DEFERENCE VARIABLE

		ENTTYPE					
		1		2		Total	
		Count	% within Deference	Count	% within Deference	Count	% within Deference
Deference	3			1	100.0%	1	100.0%
	4	1	100.0%			1	100.0%
	6	1	33.3%	2	66.7%	3	100.0%
	7	1	20.0%	4	80.0%	5	100.0%
	8	3	60.0%	2	40.0%	5	100.0%
	9	1	100.0%			1	100.0%
	10	2	40.0%	3	60.0%	5	100.0%
	11	2	50.0%	2	50.0%	4	100.0%
	12	4	100.0%			4	100.0%
	13	1	16.7%	5	83.3%	6	100.0%
	14	4	80.0%	1	20.0%	5	100.0%
	15			1	100.0%	1	100.0%
	16			1	100.0%	1	100.0%
	17			3	100.0%	3	100.0%
	18	1	100.0%			1	100.0%
	19	3	100.0%			3	100.0%
	21	1	100.0%			1	100.0%
Total		25	50.0%	25	50.0%	50	100.0%

APPENDIX X.

EPPS PSYCHOLOGICAL CHARACTERISTICS CROSS
TABULATION - DOMINANCE VARIABLE

| | | ENTTYPE | | | | | |
| | | 1 | | 2 | | Total | |
		Count	% within Dominance	Count	% within Dominance	Count	% within Dominance
Dominance	4	1	100.0%			1	100.0%
	7	2	100.0%			2	100.0%
	9	1	50.0%	1	50.0%	2	100.0%
	10			1	100.0%	1	100.0%
	11	2	66.7%	1	33.3%	3	100.0%
	12			1	100.0%	1	100.0%
	13	2	66.7%	1	33.3%	3	100.0%
	14	1	50.0%	1	50.0%	2	100.0%
	15	1	25.0%	3	75.0%	4	100.0%
	16	1	25.0%	3	75.0%	4	100.0%
	17	3	60.0%	2	40.0%	5	100.0%
	18	2	50.0%	2	50.0%	4	100.0%
	19	2	100.0%			2	100.0%
	20	3	60.0%	2	40.0%	5	100.0%
	21	2	66.7%	1	33.3%	3	100.0%
	22			3	100.0%	3	100.0%
	23	2	66.7%	1	33.3%	3	100.0%
	24			2	100.0%	2	100.0%
Total		25	50.0%	25	50.0%	50	100.0%

APPENDIX Y.

EPPS PSYCHOLOGICAL CHARACTERISTICS CROSS TABULATION - ENDURANCE VARIABLE

		ENTTYPE					
		1		2		Total	
		Count	% within Endurance	Count	% within Endurance	Count	% within Endurance
Endurance	5			1	100.0%	1	100.0%
	6			1	100.0%	1	100.0%
	9	1	33.3%	2	66.7%	3	100.0%
	10	1	33.3%	2	66.7%	3	100.0%
	11	2	40.0%	3	60.0%	5	100.0%
	12	2	100.0%			2	100.0%
	13	1	100.0%			1	100.0%
	14	2	33.3%	4	66.7%	6	100.0%
	15	2	33.3%	4	66.7%	6	100.0%
	16	2	50.0%	2	50.0%	4	100.0%
	17	2	100.0%			2	100.0%
	18	3	75.0%	1	25.0%	4	100.0%
	19	1	50.0%	1	50.0%	2	100.0%
	20	1	100.0%			1	100.0%
	21	1	100.0%			1	100.0%
	22	2	66.7%	1	33.3%	3	100.0%
	23	1	50.0%	1	50.0%	2	100.0%
	25	1	50.0%	1	50.0%	2	100.0%
	26			1	100.0%	1	100.0%
Total		25	50.0%	25	50.0%	50	100.0%

EPPS PSYCHOLOGICAL CHARACTERISTICS CROSS TABULATION - EXHIBITION VARIABLE

		ENTTYPE					
		1		2		Total	
		Count	% within Exhibition	Count	% within Exhibition	Count	% within Exhibition
Exhibition	5	1	100.0%			1	100.0%
	7			1	100.0%	1	100.0%
	10	3	100.0%			3	100.0%
	11	2	50.0%	2	50.0%	4	100.0%
	12			1	100.0%	1	100.0%
	13	2	40.0%	3	60.0%	5	100.0%
	14	2	25.0%	6	75.0%	8	100.0%
	15	5	71.4%	2	28.6%	7	100.0%
	16	3	50.0%	3	50.0%	6	100.0%
	17	1	100.0%			1	100.0%
	18			2	100.0%	2	100.0%
	19	2	40.0%	3	60.0%	5	100.0%
	20	3	60.0%	2	40.0%	5	100.0%
	26	1	100.0%			1	100.0%
Total		25	50.0%	25	50.0%	50	100.0%

APPENDIX AA.

EPPS PSYCHOLOGICAL CHARACTERISTICS CROSS TABULATION - INTRACEPTION VARIABLE

		ENTTYPE				Total	
		1		2			
		Count	% within Intraception	Count	% within Intraception	Count	% within Intraception
Intraception	6			1	100.0%	1	100.0%
	8			1	100.0%	1	100.0%
	9	1	100.0%			1	100.0%
	10	1	50.0%	1	50.0%	2	100.0%
	11	3	75.0%	1	25.0%	4	100.0%
	13	1	50.0%	1	50.0%	2	100.0%
	14	3	42.9%	4	57.1%	7	100.0%
	15	4	80.0%	1	20.0%	5	100.0%
	16	1	33.3%	2	66.7%	3	100.0%
	17	2	22.2%	7	77.8%	9	100.0%
	18	1	25.0%	3	75.0%	4	100.0%
	19	1	100.0%			1	100.0%
	20	5	71.4%	2	28.6%	7	100.0%
	21	2	66.7%	1	33.3%	3	100.0%
Total		25	50.0%	25	50.0%	50	100.0%

124

EPPS PSYCHOLOGICAL CHARACTERISTICS CROSS TABULATION - NURTURANCE VARIABLE

		ENTTYPE					
		1		2		Total	
		Count	% within Nuturance	Count	% within Nuturance	Count	% within Nuturance
Nuturance	7			1	100.0%	1	100.0%
	10	2	50.0%	2	50.0%	4	100.0%
	11	1	100.0%			1	100.0%
	12	1	50.0%	1	50.0%	2	100.0%
	13	1	50.0%	1	50.0%	2	100.0%
	14	3	75.0%	1	25.0%	4	100.0%
	15	2	40.0%	3	60.0%	5	100.0%
	16	1	50.0%	1	50.0%	2	100.0%
	17	1	20.0%	4	80.0%	5	100.0%
	18	1	50.0%	1	50.0%	2	100.0%
	19	2	33.3%	4	66.7%	6	100.0%
	20	1	50.0%	1	50.0%	2	100.0%
	21	2	100.0%			2	100.0%
	22	1	50.0%	1	50.0%	2	100.0%
	23	4	66.7%	2	33.3%	6	100.0%
	24	1	50.0%	1	50.0%	2	100.0%
	25			1	100.0%	1	100.0%
	26	1	100.0%			1	100.0%
Total		25	50.0%	25	50.0%	50	100.0%

APPENDIX CC.

EPPS PSYCHOLOGICAL CHARACTERISTICS CROSS TABULATION - ORDER VARIABLE

		ENTTYPE				Total	
		1		2			
		Count	% within Order	Count	% within Order	Count	% within Order
Order	4	1	33.3%	2	66.7%	3	100.0%
	5	3	60.0%	2	40.0%	5	100.0%
	6	2	66.7%	1	33.3%	3	100.0%
	7	3	60.0%	2	40.0%	5	100.0%
	8	1	33.3%	2	66.7%	3	100.0%
	9	1	33.3%	2	66.7%	3	100.0%
	10			3	100.0%	3	100.0%
	11	1	100.0%			1	100.0%
	12	1	50.0%	1	50.0%	2	100.0%
	13	4	80.0%	1	20.0%	5	100.0%
	14			3	100.0%	3	100.0%
	15	1	25.0%	3	75.0%	4	100.0%
	16	2	50.0%	2	50.0%	4	100.0%
	19	2	100.0%			2	100.0%
	20	1	100.0%			1	100.0%
	21	2	66.7%	1	33.3%	3	100.0%
Total		25	50.0%	25	50.0%	50	100.0%

APPENDIX DD.

EPPS PSYCHOLOGICAL CHARACTERISTICS CROSS TABULATION - SUCCORANCE VARIABLE

		ENTTYPE				Total	
		1		2			
		Count	% within Succorance	Count	% within Succorance	Count	% within Succorance
Succorance	2			1	100.0%	1	100.0%
	4			2	100.0%	2	100.0%
	5			1	100.0%	1	100.0%
	6	2	100.0%			2	100.0%
	7			2	100.0%	2	100.0%
	8	1	100.0%			1	100.0%
	9	3	50.0%	3	50.0%	6	100.0%
	10	1	50.0%	1	50.0%	2	100.0%
	11	3	50.0%	3	50.0%	6	100.0%
	12	2	40.0%	3	60.0%	5	100.0%
	13	1	100.0%			1	100.0%
	14	1	25.0%	3	75.0%	4	100.0%
	15	2	100.0%			2	100.0%
	16	2	100.0%			2	100.0%
	17	4	66.7%	2	33.3%	6	100.0%
	19			1	100.0%	1	100.0%
	20	1	25.0%	3	75.0%	4	100.0%
	21	1	100.0%			1	100.0%
	23	1	100.0%			1	100.0%
Total		25	50.0%	25	50.0%	50	100.0%

AVERAGE SCORES OF PSYCHOLOGICAL CHARACTERISTICS

	ENTTYPE								
	1			2			Total		
	Mean	n	SD	Mean	n	SD	Mean	N	SD
Abasement	15.36	25	4.33	12.80	25	4.31	14.08	50	4.47
Achievement	14.84	25	5.10	16.08	25	3.41	15.46	50	4.34
Affiliation	14.12	25	3.75	15.44	25	4.66	14.78	50	4.24
Aggression	10.16	25	5.19	11.72	25	4.43	10.94	50	4.84
Autonomy	12.16	25	4.30	15.04	25	3.97	13.60	50	4.35
Change	14.12	25	6.00	16.40	25	4.08	15.26	50	5.21
Deference	12.20	25	4.43	10.88	25	3.96	11.54	50	4.21
Dominance	15.72	25	5.21	17.20	25	4.37	16.46	50	4.82
Endurance	16.32	25	4.33	14.52	25	5.44	15.42	50	4.95
Exhibition	15.00	25	4.34	15.00	25	3.18	15.00	50	3.76
Intraception	15.84	25	3.70	15.40	25	3.64	15.62	50	3.64
Nuturance	17.72	25	4.77	17.04	25	4.55	17.38	50	4.63
Order	11.64	25	5.59	10.68	25	4.49	11.16	50	5.04
Succorance	13.40	25	4.54	11.60	25	5.24	12.50	50	4.94

ABOUT THE AUTHOR

Melissa L. Greer, Ph.D. holds a Doctorate degree in Organization & Management specializing in Information Technology from Capella University in Minneapolis, MN and a Master's degree in Business Administration. She has taught college level courses in business and computers.

She started barrel racing at the age of nine and it is her passion for horses and the barrel racing industry that led her to utilize her education in the promotion and business awareness of barrel racing competition and productions.

She currently owns and produces Florida Equine Athlete, a magazine for the barrel racers in the state of Florida, which provides story articles of different barrel racing events; informational and educational articles; calendar of events; and statistical information such as results, standings, and money winnings of many of the organizations held within the state. Dr. Greer is now producing the magazine into video broadcasts.

She also produces her own polebending and barrel racing organization and videos competitior's runs which are placed on DVD. It is a tremendous help for barrel racers in their training and/or to have for their video library.

Dr. Greer is currently working on additional books and is in the process of organizing seminars for women athletes to educate them on how to treat their sport as a business and utilize sponsorships.

Melissa was raised and continues to live in Florida. She had to take a three year break from competition so she could complete her Ph.D. studies and concentrate on business. In the meantime, she had to retire her horse that she competed on for sixteen years due to a leg injury and is currently starting another in barrel racing competition.